WINNIPEG
JAN 27 1998
WITHDRAWN
PUBLIC LIBRA

D1071644

Tubman

Harriet Tubman and the Underground Railroad

Her Life in the United States and Canada

by

Rosemary Sadlier

An UMBRELLA PRESS Publication

Toronto

Dedication

To my family for their love, patience and support.

TUBMAN: Harriet Tubman and the Underground Railroad
Her Life in the United States and Canada

Publisher: Ken Pearson
Editor: Jocelyn Smyth
Cover artist: Julie LoTauro
Design: Ron & Ron Design and Photography
Maps &Charts: Ron & Ron Design and Photography

Canadian Cataloguing in Publication Data

Sadlier, Rosemary.
Harriet Tubman and the underground railroad

(Signature series)
Includes bibliographical references and index.
ISBN 1-895642-17-5

1. Tubman, Harriet, 1820-1913 - Juvenile literature.
2. Underground railroad - Juvenile literature.
3. Slaves - United States - Biography - Juvenile literature 4. Afro-Americans - Biography - Juvenile literature.
I. Title. II. Series: Signature Series
(Toronto, Ont.)

E444.T82S33 1997 J305.5'67'092. C95-931433-4

A *kennyp* Publication

Manufactured in Canada

Published by:

UMBRELLA PRESS
56 Rivercourt Blvd.
Toronto, On. M4J 3A4

Telephone: (416) 696.6665
Fax: (416) 696.9189

Contents

Preface

I have written this book about Harriet Tubman, her achievements and contributions, because I feel that she was an international figure who has had an immeasurable impact on our concepts of freedom and justice. Tubman's heroism, spirituality, and selflessness allowed her to become one of the most famous Black women in the 19th century. Facing overwhelming odds, she managed to fend for herself and guide the 300 "passengers" in the 19 rescues she successfully executed. That she lived in Canada for eight years and that she has Canadian descendants to this day is less well known.

My cousin, the late Helen Smith, was instrumental in bringing Harriet Tubman's story to the people of St. Catharines, Ontario. It is my hope that this book will bring both the American and the Canadian story of Harriet Tubman to a wider audience and provide further insight about this remarkable woman.

I was drawn to this project because I have been touched by the accomplishments of this heroic woman who had no social, educational, or financial advantages because of her birth, race, and gender. Clearly, if she could make a difference, we can too.

I wish to acknowledge the contributions of all those who so kindly provided ideas, documents, pictures, oral histories and referrals which have helped me in the research and writing of this book, particularly the following in both the United States and Canada:

Nancy Assman, historian, Cayuga County, Auburn, New York
Gail Benjafield, St. Catharines Public Library, St. Catharines, Ontario
John Bertniak, Archives, Brock University, St. Catharines, Ontario
Charles Blockson, curator, Afro-American Collection Temple University, Philadelphia, Pennsylvania
Dorchester Public Library, Cambridge, Maryland
Pat Fraser, St. Catharines, Ontario
Malcolm Goodelle, Archivist, Cayuga County Historian
Dr. Daniel G. Hill, Toronto, Ontario
Calvin Kimbrough, Niagara University, Buffalo, New York
Paul Litt, Ontario Heritage Foundation, Toronto, Ontario
Ed Patton, Western New York Heritage Centre, Buffalo, New York
Arden Phair, St. Catharines Museum, St. Catharines, Ontario
Michael Power, Welland, Ontario
Paul Redding, Kenicious College, Niagara Falls, New York
Helen Smith, Salem Chapel, BME Church, St. Catharines, Ontario
Susan Suk, St. Catharines, Ontario

Owen Thomas, Brantford, Ontario
Judy Tye, Toronto, Ontario
Glen Walker, Fort Erie, Ontario
Sheila Wilson, St. Catharines Public Library, St. Catharines, Ontario

Many descendants of Harriet Tubman shared their time and their stories with me. I would like to thank everyone who unveiled the story of the descendants of Harriet Tubman, in particular:

Betty Browne, Dundas, Ontario
Geraldine Copes, Rochester, New York
Pauline Copes Johnson, Rochester, New York
Laberta Greenlea, Rochester, New York
Joyce Jones, Syracuse, New York
Hazel Martin, Buffalo, New York
Mariline Wilkins, Philadelphia, Pennsylvania
. . . and their children, grandchildren and great-grandchildren.

I would like to acknowledge the financial support of the Writing and Publication program of Multiculturalism Program of the Department of Canadian Heritage.

Through my mother's family, I am a descendant of those who made their way to Canada through the Underground Railroad. Because of this I am particularly interested in the courage of these people and how they came to be free. Unfortunately, I am deeply aware of how little information is known about the systems they used. Despite the importance of passing this heritage down through the generations to the contemporary Black community, particularly through oral tradition, many personal experiences of freedom seekers remain hidden forever.

Harriet Tubman was committed to helping her family and this prompted her to carry out several crossings to rescue her relatives. I wondered if perhaps within the fabric of the stories of the Tubman family there would be details that would extend our knowledge of Harriet and the secret routes she used? Or, if perhaps her legacy had lived on through the presence of her descendants? Because the descendants might hold the answer to some of the missing pieces, I began a study of Tubman's family legacy, as well as her own historical legacy. I met with many descendants from both the United States and Canada and I have included a section on Harriet's North American genealogy, reflecting her family in both the United States and Canada.

I feel that information of her family and descendants is important to our understanding of Tubman, the Underground Railroad and the settlement of people of African descent. It is important for all those who made the run for freedom and never arrived; for those buried in forgotten or hidden cemeteries without our knowledge; and for those of us, like Harriet, who realize that one person can make a difference.

Rosemary Sadlier
Toronto

Introduction

Harriet Tubman was born a slave on a plantation near Bucktown, Maryland, sometime about the year 1820. There are no official records of her birth because it was not thought to be important enough to keep such records for slaves. Today, she is considered to be one of the most famous conductors on the Underground Railroad – if not one of the most famous people of her time. Through her leadership and determination, she guided some 300 enslaved Black people to their freedom through the network known as the Underground Railroad.

The economy of the United States, especially in the agricultural south, was built upon the labour of captured Africans. Slavery, as experienced by the survivors of the "Middle Passage" between Africa and the New World, and their descendants, was all encompassing. They had no rights whatsoever under the law. Black slaves had to work constantly under the watchful eye of an overseer who whipped slow workers. They could not legally marry and raise a family. They could not attend school or learn to read and write. They could not live where they wished, follow their interests or move about in society as they pleased. Unlike the slavery imposed by other societies, at other times, they were slaves for life. If children came about through forced acts of breeding, love or violence, they were automatically enslaved. And, because Africans had distinctive dark complexions in a society in which free people were white, their skin colour immediately identified them as being slaves. Their African names, religions, histories, languages, customs, and families were taken from them by the time they were auctioned off. They were required to use the name given to them by their owner. They were forced to work hard, for which they received no salary and little recognition.

Over time, and for various reasons – the owner's guilty conscience, a slave's decreased value because of old age or poor health; or attitude changes to slave owning – certain slaves were granted their freedom. The northern states, with their large Quaker settlements and anti-slavery proponents tended to free slaves earlier than other areas. This pressured neighbouring states and Canada to struggle with the debate about abolishing slavery or continuing it.

In 1793, the cotton gin was invented and became widely used. It permitted the plantation owner, through the work of his slaves, to more quickly and efficiently remove the tiny seeds from cotton. This resulted in much more profit for the owners. By 1793, the first Fugitive Slave Law in the United States came into force and allowed slave owners or their agents – bounty hunters or slave catchers – to bring any Black person before a magistrate, accused of being a runaway. With the vague descrip-

Harriet Tubman in mid-life.

tions of freedom-seeking slaves that existed, any Black person who was so accused was forced to be returned to the "master." Because the free labour of the slaves was so valuable to their owners and to the agricultural economy of the South, the White Southerner plantation owner relied on exploiting the labour of slaves.

In Canada, the first known slave, Olivier Le Jeune, a young boy, was brought into Canada in 1628. Slaves were held in Canada only by the wealthy to do household work, livery work, barbering and laundry. Large-scale plantations did not exist in the country, so there were fewer slaves. It was not until 1834 that slavery was abolished in the British Empire, including Canada.

Black people did not want to be slaves and fought against it as well as they could. They passively resisted (intentionally

The slave quarters shown in this drawing are significantly more attractive than the actual quarters the slaves had to live in.

working extra slowly, pretending not to understand commands, discreetly contaminating or poisoning food), and many slave revolts are documented. However, trying to run away was extremely difficult and they would be tracked down like animals by groups of men with guns and dogs. If caught alive, they would be returned to their master and punishment might be the loss of a foot, an ear or a hand, or by a severe whipping, leaving the freedom seeker able to work but likely unable to attempt another escape. It also signalled to other would-be runaways the punishment they could expect for trying to leave. When it was easy to obtain slaves, the runaway might be hanged, but as the importation of Africans slowed down in the late eighteenth century, and was abolished in the United States in 1808, torture, branding, disfigurement and maiming were preferred to destroying "property." Stolen labour was so valued by owners of large plantations that in Virginia in the 1850s officials even considered enslaving "poor Whites." Human dignity and free choice were unimportant especially when wealth could be amassed by dehumanizing and exploiting others.

Slaves lived in separate shacks away from the big house – mansion – where the owner lived. Their "homes" had dirt floors and possibly one thin blanket for a bed. Meals were plain – cornmeal porridge and fish would be served from a pot and eaten with hands. The stolen "discards" from slaughtered pigs and cows would supplement their rations. The discards consisted of heads, intestines, organs, feet and tails, and squirrels or other small animals might be caught by industrious, hungry Black people. Some tended their own vegetable patches near their quarters. If the slaves became ill, they had to nurse themselves back to health as no doctor would be summoned for them. Herbal remedies from the African tradition or learned from Native People were indeed valuable. Mothers might be able to have their children with them in the evenings, but even children were taken into the master's house to assist or were hired out to work for others at the whim of their owner.

Parents and children, brothers and sisters, husbands and wives could at any time be permanently separated from each other by being sold. In fact, some owners felt that people of African descent had no feelings, and did not care if their children were taken from them. Pro-slavery forces felt that enslaved Africans accepted and actually preferred to live their lives in bondage.

There was little comfort for slaves except each other. Work might slow down on Sundays as Christian owners and overseers would not work that day. Religion was used to reinforce the slaves "inferior" position and justify their abuse. If a slave died, he or she could only be buried at night because the master's needs for the labour of his slaves always came first, well above the emotional trauma felt by the slave community over loosing a loved one. The images of freedom and movement in many of the hymns they sang did help to provide images of a life that might be in the North or after death. In time, those hymns became codes for people who were willing to follow the call to freedom.

The Underground Railroad was born of the desperation and resolve of Black people to be free, and the commitment and resources of free Blacks and Whites to end slavery. The Underground Railroad was the name given to the means used by escaping slaves to achieve freedom through the trails, safe houses and various methods of transportation. It was a system

Lake Superior
Lake Huron
Lake Michigan
Lake Ontario
Lake Erie
QUEBEC
Montreal
Ottawa
MAINE
VERMONT
NEW HAMPSHIRE
ONTARIO
NEW YORK
MICHIGAN
Toronto
Syracuse
Auburn
Rochester
Albany
Boston
MASSACHUSETTS
St. Catharines
Buffalo
Hartford
RI
Providence
CONNECTICUT
RHODE ISLAND
Newark
New York City
PENNSYLVANIA
Cleveland
Philadelphia
NEW JERSEY
OHIO
Atlantic City
Dover
MARYLAND
DELAWARE
Washington
Columbus
Annapolis
INDIANA
Cincinnati
WEST VIRGINIA
Bucktown
ILLINOIS
Richmond
VIRGINIA
Norfolk
KENTUCKY
NORTH CAROLINA
Charlotte
TENNESSEE
SOUTH CAROLINA
Charleston
MISSISSIPPI
ALABAMA
GEORGIA
Savannah
Atlantic Ocean
N
FLORIDA
Gulf of Mexico

of people helping people to be free, but it was extremely dangerous. The Underground Railroad "carried" its human cargo from the early 1800s until slavery was abolished in the United States beginning in 1863. It was most active in the period following the passing of the second Fugitive Slave Act in 1850. Through this Act, all Blacks, whether free born, manumitted (granted their freedom in the Will of their owner) or runaway, were at risk of recapture no matter where they were in the United States. Many of these Blacks had been free for several generations and had acquired considerable property, but if they resisted being re-enslaved they were beaten or killed.

A "ride" on the Underground Railroad would not be comfortable. Your conductor would lead you north on foot by night, through swamps, paths, river shores, and forests. If you were lucky, you would have part of your passage on a real train or boat paid for or provided by abolitionists. You might have to wear a disguise, although you still ran the risk of sitting beside someone who could identify you. You might travel from one station to another in a secret wagon compartment or on a makeshift boat. Your food would consist of whatever you had been able to carry and whatever you could find – nuts, berries, roots or donated goods – during the six to nine weeks your trip could take to get to safety. Along the way, your sleeping quarters might be a hollow tree, a culvert under a bridge, a cemetery, a root cellar, a barn, a cave or the open terrain. Until you reached your final destination, you would be in constant fear of being recaptured. Many died along the way or soon after reaching the land of freedom because of starvation, chronic fatigue or exposure. Before 1850, you only needed to travel to the northern United States, but with the passage of the second Fugitive Slave Act in 1850, your trip would have to be longer, all the way to Canada. Therefore, the risk of recapture would be greater. You would "buy" your Underground Railroad ticket with your commitment to be free at any cost, including leaving your family behind, and you would "claim" your luggage of liberty with your first steps into Canada.

Journey to Freedom

[A Fictional Account]

Harriet Tubman was silently making her way north with a group of 25 escaping slaves in the early morning. They were all hungry and tired, and now the heavens had opened up, dropping sheets of rain on the brave group. Only the twin baby girls were oblivious to their circumstances – Harriet had given them a sleeping drug to make sure they stayed quiet.

Suddenly, a feeble light appeared, flickering from the window of what they could barely make out as a cottage. It was the safe house Harriet had promised they would reach. The prospect of some food and shelter from the rain lifted their spirits, and some of the group wanted to run ahead to hug the members of the free black family that lived there. They were so hungry that even a stale crust of bread would seem like the most wonderful meal in the world!

But Harriet warned them to be quiet, to stay hidden where they were and to remain motionless. Even though she had been welcomed at the safe house before, she knew she had to always be on guard for bounty hunters who were everywhere. She heard the yelp of the hounds and sensed that something was not quite as it should be. Maybe it was the way the lamp was placed in the window – usually it was in the centre of the window, but tonight it wasn't.

Cautiously, Harriet approached the door of the cottage and knocked in her special way to give the secret signal. After a time, a White man opened the door and demanded to know what she wanted. Harriet had to think fast. If she didn't give him some reasonable answer, he would surely be suspicious. She was looking for a friend of hers, she said. The man replied that her friend no longer lived there, that he had been obliged to leave because he had been involved in helping slaves escape. Harriet thanked him for the information and quickly turned away.

Harriet knew that it would be only a matter of moments before the man realized that she might be a runaway slave seeking shelter. When he did realize this, he would certainly alert others who would come looking for her and her charges with horses and wagons, even dogs.

Dawn was fast approaching when Harriet suddenly remembered that there was a small island in the middle of a nearby swamp, with tall grass that would conceal them. The exhausted party waded to the island and Harriet ordered them to lie down in the grass. They obeyed, knowing that their very lives depended on following her instructions. Harriet considered going off by herself to find food as they hadn't eaten a patrolling the area looking for them. What to do?

She decided not to risk exposing the group. The deeply religious Harriet began a silent prayer, hoping and expecting that in due course the needs of her charges, would be taken care of. All through the morning and afternoon, she prayed. Finally, at dusk, a man dressed like a Quaker walked slowly along the pathway just across from where her frightened group huddled still and quiet. He seemed to be talking to himself, and as he got closer, Harriet heard him say, "My wagon stands in the barnyard of the next farm across the way. The horse is in the stable, the harness hangs on a nail." He then continued on his way.

When darkness fell, Harriet left the group to investigate the farm the man had mentioned and discovered that indeed the horse and wagon were there, along with a good supply of food, which had been placed in the wagon. She quickly gathered her passengers together in the wagon and made her way to the nearby town. There, another Underground Railroad station-master helped her and the group on the next leg of their journey to freedom to the North.

Chapter One

The Underground Railroad

The Underground Railroad is described by some as the first freedom movement in North America. It brought people of diverse backgrounds together for a common purpose, and freed enslaved people of African descent.

The Underground Railroad was not a real train or tunnel leading to freedom. It was a system of people helping people to become free. Formerly enslaved people, human cargo, were transported to a series of safe destinations until they were in an area that supported their right to be free. Many were guided by the North Star since they travelled by night and rested by day to avoid detection. But more than anything else, they had a strong desire to live in freedom, and their own courage led them to board the "Freedom Train," the Underground Railroad.

Those who helped enslaved people were White, Black or Native people; they were Quakers or just people committed to helping. This cooperative system brought enslaved Africans from slave-holding southern states into "free," non-slave holding northern states and later into Canada. With the end of the importation of people from Africa to the United States in 1808, there were no new slaves to replace any who had escaped, except for the children of already captive people. Instead, those enslaved Africans who had escaped were hunted down and returned to their owners. Bounty hunters came into northern, industrial states in search of escaped slaves and hence to the attention of abolitionists.

The Underground Railroad got its name in the 1840s from a frustrated slave owner who had been trying to capture runaway slaves. At a point along the Ohio River when the freedom seekers just seemed to disappear, he exclaimed, "Those abolitionists must have a railroad somewhere under ground." The term "Underground" was, therefore, coined and it continued to be used for over twenty years, even though there had been escapes into Canada for decades before the 1840s.

The escapes of enslaved American people into Canada started before the term was used – before a system had really developed. The Underground Railroad, however, was underground in the sense that it was secret or hidden from common knowledge, and it was a railroad because it seemed to be as swift and efficient a means of transportation as the actual trains and railroad lines that were being built at the time. Railroad terms were used to both confuse bounty hunters and slave owners and to describe people and places connected to this secret means of moving people from enslavement to liberty.

As a slave you had no rights under the law. You were forced to work from dawn until dusk doing whatever was required by the master. The economy of the South was based on agriculture; the profitable production of agriculture depended on exploiting the free labour of enslaved people to do the back-breaking work of clearing, weeding, planting, tending, and harvesting crops of sugar, rice, cotton or tobacco. At any time, you could be sold and moved away from your family and friends. You could be whipped or beaten or even killed, all at the whim of the person who owned you. Being enslaved meant that you were not free to do what you wanted or to go where you pleased because you were not considered to have any needs that were important. You were often viewed virtually as a mere beast of burden. According to law, an enslaved person of African descent did not even have status as a "person."

In 1793, Eli Whitney invented the cotton gin, a machine that separated the fibre from the seeds of cotton. Previously, slaves would have the task of separating by hand the cotton from the tiny seeds in the centre of each cotton boll, a very difficult and time consuming job. With the invention of the cotton gin, this was done quickly and cotton could be sold ready to create fabric or garments in a far shorter time. In fact, this operation of separating the fibre from the seed could be done 50 times faster than in the past. With this increased production came an increased demand for cotton and the need to cultivate and process cotton on a large scale. In only ten years after Whitney's invention, the value of the cotton crop in the United States alone increased from about $150 000 to over $8 million. By 1840, "King Cotton," as it was called, made up over 60 percent of American exports; it also led, however, to an

Underground Railroad Terms

The terms used for the Underground Railroad came into use about the year 1840, although slaves had been escaping north before this time. The mid–1800s was a period in which railroads were being constructed in North America as well as elsewhere in the world. Railroad terms seemed appropriate to signal the various aspects of secrecy surrounding the Underground Railroad – and to confuse slave catchers. The following are some of the terms used:

Conductor: A person who would guide freedom seekers from one station to another along a track of the Underground Railroad.

Drinking Gourd: The North Star was referred to as the "Drinking Gourd." The North Star had a constant position in the sky and could be depended upon to provide direction for people at night during their travel.

Freedom Seekers: Enslaved Africans who were determined to be free.

Passengers, Cargo or Freight: The coded terms that referred to runaway slaves.

Station: A safe house or area where freedom seekers could find food and / or shelter. In many cases the escapee would hide in a root cellar or a hidden room or barn. Although there was no master plan, stations were often located about 25 kilometres apart.

Station Master: The person who would watch out for freedom seekers, provide them with clothing and food and give them information on the route the freedom seekers should follow on the next stage of their journey.

Stockholders: People who helped freedom seekers by donating money, food, clothing or any item that could be used.

Terminal: The final destination of the freedom seekers.

Track: A route on the Underground Railroad.

Underground Railroad and Crossing to Canada

The Underground Railroad transported its human cargo in many ways. Walking was the primary means of transportation since they could travel in remote areas at night and according to their needs. Although not planned, stations were generally about 25 kilometres apart. If train passes were obtained secretly. Disguised fugitives would then travel as if they were affluent and free Blacks. At one point, the Grand Trunk Railroad openly charged fugitives half fare or allowed them to board with a pass. However, others had to be cloistered with the luggage or livestock.

Freedom seekers were guided by land and water routes to terminals in Canada, such as St. Catharines, Hamilton, Toronto, Brantford, Windsor, Amherstburg, Kingston and Prescott. This was a time of side-wheel paddle steamers on the Great Lakes and Blacks could board these in Rochester and travel to St. Catharines or Toronto.

Harriet Tubman regularly stopped in Rochester for assistance and a brief rest provided by contacts of Frederick Douglass. They might be hidden in Williamston, transported in a wagon with a false bottom to the docks of Puttneyville and on to Niagara Falls by boat and their freedom.

increased need for slave labour, particularly in the southern states. The owners put more pressure on their slaves to work and they became more opposed to any anti-slavery measures and legislation.

The penalties for trying to escape became even more severe for both the slaves and the abolitionists who helped them. The invention of the cotton gin increased the need for slaves and increased the justification to keep people of African descent as slaves. Despite a fondness for Black mammies, their nannies, or the intimacy between slaves and owners, a troubling perspective took hold, helping southern plantation owners to see only with racist eyes. It was easier to keep your slaves and mistreat them when the culture, politics, economy, religion and every aspect of society supported the view that African people were inferior, unworthy and incapable of supporting themselves. On this basis, some people argued that slavery was not an evil. This was when a dark skin was supposedly evidence of inferiority.

Enslaved Africans abhorred being slaves and fought against it as best they could. There are many records of violent slave uprisings. Each time a revolt occurred, the laws would be changed to make it more difficult for an organized resistance movement to gain strength again. This left few options available to people who were opposed to their bondage. Slaves would passively resist by doing tasks slower or pretending not to understand what needed to be done, all the while monitoring the reaction of the overseer to avoid punishment. Male slaves had greater opportunities to experience life outside the plantation through running errands for the master in neighbouring areas. It was common to see Black enslaved men taking care of the master or his business concerns. It would be hard to hold young Black men familiar with outdoor life, who might have learned how to travel to where freedom was a possibility.

This is a portrayal of the end of a hard day's work in the field. These field workers had to meet quotas of produce during their 10- to 12-hour days.

Black women tended not to run away simply because they were more closely watched, often working in or near the home of the master, preparing food, doing laundry or tending the vegetable garden. They may not have had the opportunity to explore the surrounding area of the plantation and therefore lacked the outdoor skills that would sustain them in the wild. They might have the task of caring for the master's children or tending to an elderly or sick person, the type work that demanded the constant presence of the enslaved woman. Or they themselves could be pregnant or not well enough to consider a major trek when speed was critical to the success of the escape. However, since Black women often were closer to the home of the master, they were in a good position to overhear the plans of the master and to inform others.

Description reads: The undersigned wishes to purchase a large lot of Negroes for the New Orleans market. I will pay $1200 to $1250 for No.1 young men and $830 to $1000 for No.1 young women.

If the sounds of a spiritual seemed to be sung over and over again, starting at one plantation and spreading to another, there may have been a message that was being conveyed. The spiritual might be "Wade in the Water" or "Go Down Moses" or "Get on Board, Little Children." The proper lyrics sung at the right time would let other slaves know that an escape was about to take place. Or a glance or a look or some other body language would let only those who needed to know determine that you might be about to make yourself free. When everyone knew an escape was about to happen, without asking, they would know that they had to divert the attention of the master or to make sure that he had lots of brandy to drink in the evening. The laws and customs of slavery gave the owner the right to demand absolute obedience and work from his slaves. Patrols of volunteers routinely watched the roads and known crossings points, watching for a Black person who would be assumed to be escaping. Bounty hunters actually tracked escapees with dogs, bringing back the fugitive slave dead or alive – whatever was easier or would bring the most money to the bounty hunter.

Abolitionists

Abolitionists were people who were strongly opposed to slavery on humanitarian, religious or political grounds. An abolitionist might be a former slave owner who had come to realize that the exploitation of others was unacceptable in any society. An abolitionist might be a Black person who had been enslaved and knew the terrors of slavery or a White person who had to do whatever could be done to rid this injustice. Certain religious groups were active abolitionists, including the Quakers. Abolitionists were activists who were frequently concerned with women's rights, temperance, and peace initiatives in addition to their anti-slavery work.

Hidden Messages

Hidden messages were coded in spirituals that were sung by slaves, but eventually owners found out about the purpose of these and forbid the slaves from singing them. The spiritual, "Go Down Moses" could not be sung by Blacks in the South, particularly as Harriet was known as the "Moses of her people," but it is a beautiful song full of the indignation of enslaved people:

"Oh go down Moses,
Way down into Egypt's land
Tell old Pharaoh
Let my people go.

Oh, Pharaoh said he would go cross,
Let my people go,
And don't get lost in the wilderness,
Let my people go.

Oh, go down Moses,
Way down into Egypt's land,
Tell old Pharaoh,
Let my people go.

You may hinder me here, but you can't up there,
Let my people go,
He sits in the Heaven and answers prayer,
Let my people go.

Oh, go down Moses,
Way down into Egypt's land,
Tell old Pharaoh,
Let my people go."

Others feel that Harriet's success in rescuing slaves may have inspired the spiritual "Swing Low, Sweet Chariot". The chorus suggests that freedom will be yours if you get on board.

"Swing Low, sweet chariot
Coming for to carry me home.
Swing low, sweet chariot,
Coming for to carry me home."

The Underground Railroad had many dedicated and caring people involved with it, including the Canadian abolitionist, Dr. Alexander Milton Ross. Dr. Ross used his bird-watching hobby as an excuse to travel to slave-holding states and while there to arrange time alone with the slaves to tell them of escape routes. Numerous Canadian and American abolitionists established anti-slavery societies to collect money for the transportation, feeding or clothing of freedom seekers. Free Black abolitionists formed vigilance societies which patrolled the community looking for runaways in order to offer them shelter. On the other hand, there were also people, like Patty Canon from New England, who tricked escaping slaves. By acting as if she would shelter the refugee, Canon thereby gained their trust, but, in fact, she would lure them to their capture and death.

Blacks who had fought in the American War of Independence or the War of 1812 might have become familiar with Canada and the freedom that was possible in the North. As determined as Black people were to be free, there were also abolitionists and many Quakers who were equally determined to do what they could to free slaves. The sight of self-emancipated Black people, runaway slaves, being hunted down or shot near the dwellings of non-slave owners in the North brought the inhumanity of slavery home to them. People in the North could no longer view slavery as a condition affecting only the South: it touched everyone.

It is believed that the Underground Railroad may have begun early in the 1800s in Pennsylvania, where many Quakers lived. Coincidentally, the stations of the Underground Railroad tended to be 25-30 kilometres apart – about the distance between the meeting halls of the Quakers. Philadelphia, with its large Quaker population and growing free Black settlement, also became an active

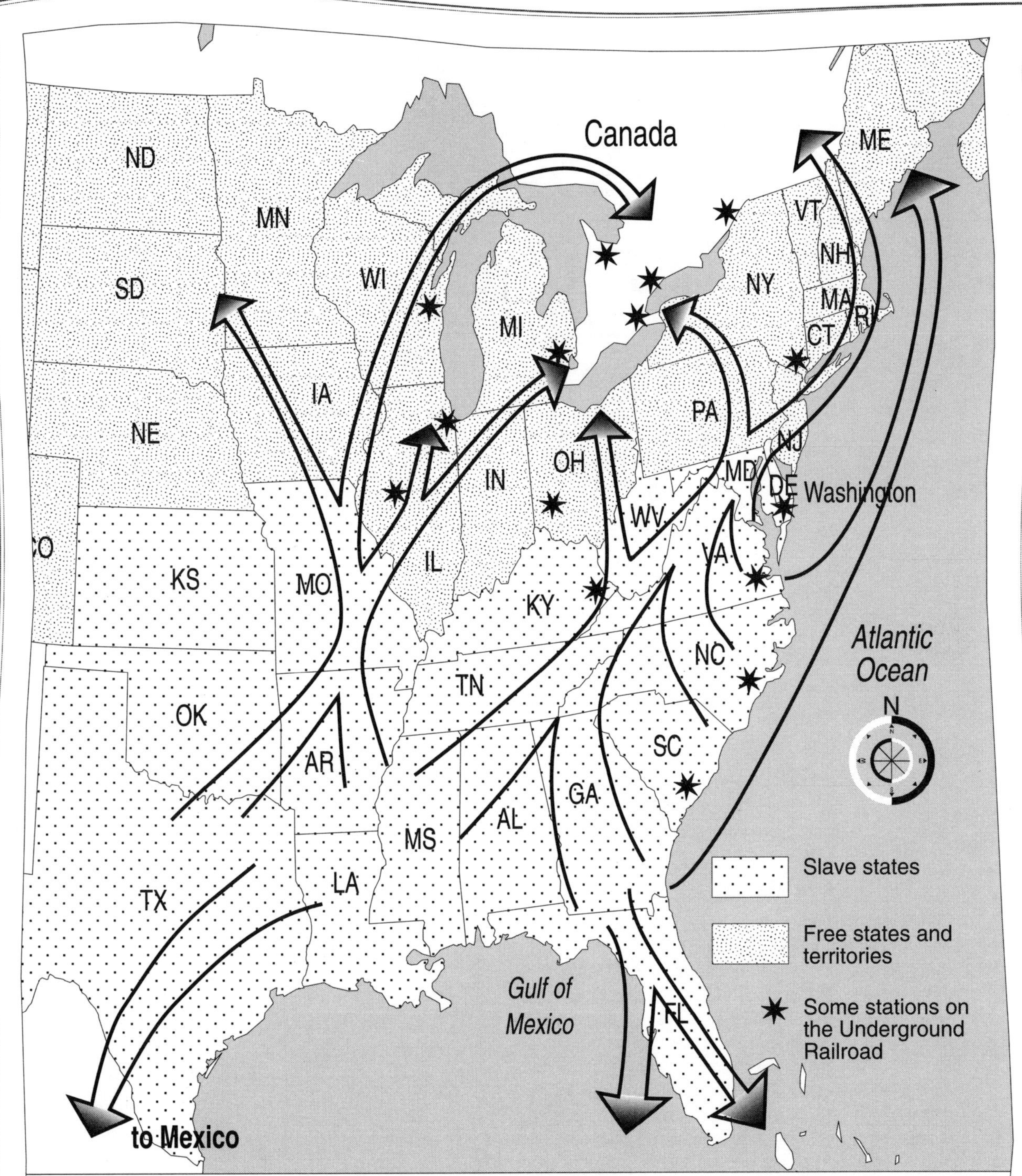

Underground Railroad stations, routes to freedom, and a final terminus. The Niagara Black History Association gives tours through Niagara's "Freedom Trail." The sites include the British Methodist Episcopal (BME) Church in St. Catharines which was the place of worship for Harriet Tubman and the Canadian headquarters of the Underground Railroad; the Nathaniel Dett Memorial Chapel (named in honour of a man born in Chatham who became an internationally renowned musician and composer); a safe house in Fort Erie; and the Norval Johnson Heritage Library in Niagara Falls, home to a growing collection of Canadian Black history books.

This drawing illustrates a stereotypical re-enslavement by bounty hunters and the prejudices of the artist.

haven. Some Quakers, such as Levi Coffin, gained experience moving people along the Railroad. He became the "President" of the Underground Railroad because of his central role in the movement in the Cincinnati, Ohio, area.

Ohio was an area ripe for moving human cargo because a number of restrictive laws required free Blacks to produce court-issued papers. These laws, known as Black Codes, prevented Blacks without this documentation from working or settling in the state. Clearly, a person who had just made his or her way from a southern plantation would not have this legal certificate. Such persons would obviously have few choices: remain in Ohio unable to support themselves, return to the plantation in the South, or journey across the border into Canada.

By the 1820s the force of restrictive laws in other states, as well as the support for the freedom of Black people in Canada, encouraged the development of Underground Railroad routes from states such as Michigan, Ohio, Indiana, New York, Virginia, Maryland and Delaware into Canada. In just one province of Canada (present-day Ontario) some major terminals included Windsor, Amherstburg, Chatham, Niagara Falls, Fort Erie, St. Catharines, Hamilton, Brantford, London, Toronto, Owen Sound, and Collingwood. In 1833, an Act of the British Parliament abolished slavery throughout the British Empire, including Canada. This Act, effective August 1, 1834, solidified Canada's position as a possible haven for freedom seekers. Although some slaves escaped to Mexico or the West Indies, Canada was closer, more accessible, growing rapidly, and a place where all peoples' rights were protected under the law. Slaves travelling to Canada with their masters would know about freedom there, as would informed American abolitionists.

Fugitive Slave Act of 1850

The Fugitive Slave Act of 1850 made it legal for anyone, anywhere in the United States to accuse any Black person of being an escaped slave. It brought all of the powers of the state to bear on returning "property" to the owner of the slave. Importation of Africans had been outlawed since 1808 in the United States, making it more difficult for southern plantation owners to maintain their supply of free labour, especially when many slaves were running away. Under this law, when a Black person was captured he/she was then processed by a commissioner who, in fact, would make more money if he ruled in favour of the slave holder than if he ruled in favour of freedom for the Black person. This was the second Fugitive Slave Act passed to appease the interests of the slave-holding South which accused the northern free states of harbouring runaways since the passing of the original and weaker Fugitive Slave Act of 1793.

The Fugitive Slave Act of 1850 was the major catalyst to push people into action as abolitionists, Underground Railroad workers or freedom seekers. This law brought all of the power of the state to bear on returning actual or accused runaway slaves back to southern plantations. Both the free Black and the enslaved population fled to Canada, often with the aid of the Underground Railroad. While figures for the number of Black people who travelled on the Underground Railroad vary widely, from 25 000 to 60 000 – mainly because it was a secret movement – a significant number came to Canada, stopping the flight only with the beginning of the Civil War and the ensuing abolition of slavery in 1863-1865.

Travel or involvement with the Underground Railroad was risky business. If you were caught escaping slavery, you were in violation of the law and committing a serious crime because you were stealing your valuable labour from the master who owned you. A "runaway" could have an ear cropped off, part of a foot removed, be severely whipped or even killed as a lesson to others who dreamed of escape and freedom. Non-slaves involved with the Underground Railroad could have their property seized or destroyed, be imprisoned, be tarred and feathered, fined or murdered.

Some courageous people devoted their lives to freeing others despite these significant risks. The longing to be free was stronger than the fear of capture for many thousands who made their way to Canada. As the closest English-speaking country, with a climate similar to the northern United States, Canada was accessible on foot or by small rafts or boats. As a country that had laws granting and protecting the freedom of enslaved persons, Canada would have seemed like the promised land to many.

Simcoe and Abolition of Slavery

Mattieu da Costa, the first known Black person in Canada, arrived as a free Black in 1603. He acted as an interpreter between the Micmac and the French about 1605. Slavery was introduced by the French in 1628 and continued by the British. Slavery became a status symbol as only the elite from business, the church or the military could afford to own a slave.

At the end of the American Revolutionary war, supporters of the British side, the Loyalists, were allowed to bring their slaves and belongings to Canada. Some British supporters were Black Loyalists who were granted their freedom in exchange for their service in the war. The War of 1812 also brought another group of Black veterans to Canada.

In 1793, John Graves Simcoe became the first Lieutenant-Governor of Upper Canada (now Ontario).

Earlier, Simcoe had been a supporter of political reformer and abolitionist William Wilberforce in England. When he was appointed to his position of Governor of Upper Canada, he, along with Chief Justice William Osgoode and Attorney-General John White, introduced a bill to the Legislative Assembly to make a start to end slavery. Although he introduced an abolition bill, the opposition of slave-owning legislators reduced the bill to prohibit the importation of slaves, making Ontario the first British territory to legislate against slavery. The new law also freed the children born of slaves by their twenty-fifth birthday. However, it was not until the passage of the British Imperial Act of 1833, effective August 1, 1834, by the British parliament that slavery was finally ended in Canada.

300 DOLLARS

REWARD!

RUNAWAY from John S. Doak on the 21st inst., two NEGRO MEN; LOGAN 45 years of age, bald-headed, one or more crooked fingers; DAN 21 years old, six feet high. Both black.

I will pay ONE HUNDRED DOLLARS for the apprehension and delivery of LOGAN, or to have him confined so that I can get him.

I will also pay TWO HUNDRED DOLLARS for the apprehension of DAN, or to have him confined so that I can get him.

JOHN S. DOAKE.

Springfield, Mo., April 24th, 1857.

When capturing new Africans to be slaves was banned, every effort was made to retrieve "stolen property," Africans already enslaved in the United States.

Chapter Two

Harriet's Early Life as a Slave

Harriet Ross Tubman was one of the youngest of the 11 children born to Benjamin Ross (Ben) and Araminta (Rittia or "Rit") Green Ross. Because both her parents were slaves, she was born a slave. Her mother, Rit, was owned by a Maryland plantation owner named Edward Brodas (sometimes spelled Brodess), and her father, Ben, was owned by another person, Dr. Thompson. Two of Harriet's great-grandparents had been members of the Ashanti tribe in Africa and had been captured and transported from Central Ghana about 1725. Harriet was the fourth generation of her family to be enslaved in the United States.

Young enslaved children were cared for by slaves who were too old to do more strenuous work. Once a year the slaves were issued their clothes, and Harriet received her rough cotton smock, but nothing else, just like the other slave children. No shoes were given to slaves, and Rit, like the other enslaved adults, received plain outfits or the used clothes of the master's family and his staff. To keep warm on chilly nights, Harriet would snuggle up to her mother as they, along with the rest of the family, tried to sleep on the dirt floor of the tiny place reserved for them as a home. Many children were sold away from their parents and never knew what happened to their parents or brothers and sisters. Harriet, however, had the benefit of warm nurturing parents and the security of being in the same place as her family. Over time, slaves knew little of their African heritage and little of their family background. At least Harriet had some knowledge of hers.

Experiences as a Slave

When Harriet was about five years old, Edward Brodas hired her out to other people, who would pay him for her services. As was the custom for slaves, she took another name when she was hired out, calling herself Araminta or "Minty."

One of the times she was hired out she was only five-years old and she had to clean the house all day and sit on the floor throughout the night and rock the owner's baby. Because she was a slave, her own need for sleep was not considered. If the baby cried and awakened the mistress, Harriet was beaten. She dusted and swept to the best of her ability, but as a five-year old her best was not good enough. She was whipped about her face, neck and back four times before her mistress finally realized that the child needed to be shown how to do these tasks properly. As a result, for the rest of her life, Harriet bore the marks of these and later beatings, and until the day she died, she detested indoor work and slavery.

Harriet received no education and throughout her life could not read or write. And yet in later life she gave speeches in support of women's rights, emancipation and temperance.

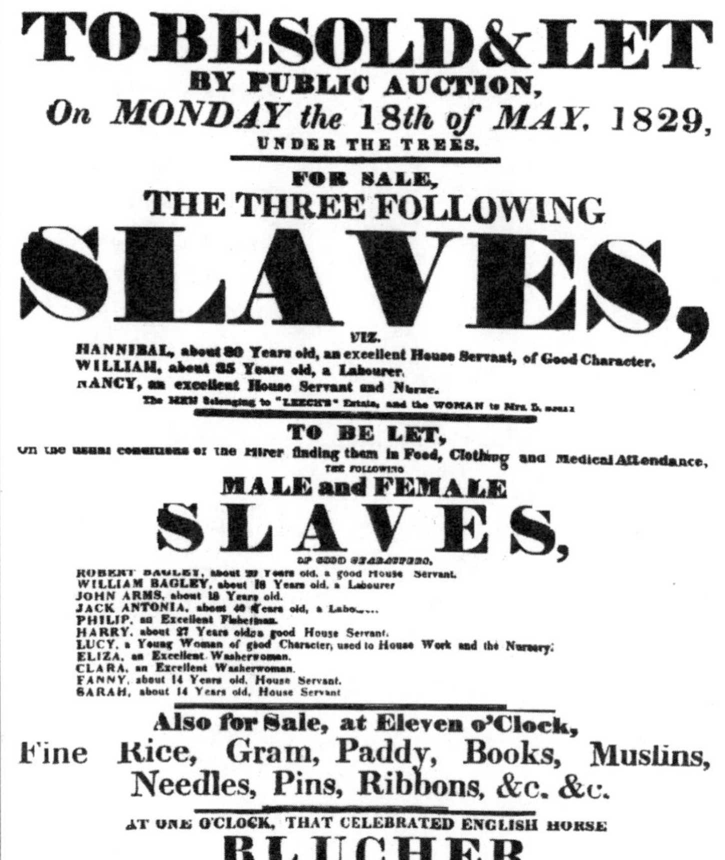

On a later job, Harriet learned to weave, but the fibres in the air from the cotton bothered her. Since she couldn't do this work, the master, James Cook, then had her tend his muskrat traps in the nearby Greenbriar swamp. This pleased Harriet as she preferred to be outdoors, away from the watchful eye of the mistress, but she soon became sick and feverish because of the insects and dampness of the swamp. In spite of her illness, her master insisted she keep working, but when Harriet was unable to continue, she was returned to her mother to regain her strength. Rit's knowledge of helpful herbs and her almost constant care got Harriet through her bouts of measles and pneumonia – she had to tend her as no doctors would be available for slaves. Harriet later said that Brodas, her owner, was not unnecessarily cruel but that those to whom she was hired out, such as Cook, were "tyrannical and brutal."

Appears like I prayed all the time, about my work, everywhere; I was always talking to the Lord. When I went to the horse-trough to wash my face, and took up the water in my hands, I said, 'Oh, Lord, wash me, make me clean.' When I took up the towel to wipe my face and hands, I cried, 'Oh, Lord, for Jesus' sake, wipe away my sins!' When I took up the broom and began to sweep, I groaned, 'Oh, Lord, whatsoever sin there be in my heart, sweep it out, Lord, clear and clean,' but I can't pray no more for poor old master.

Harriet was deprived of many of the things that her owners took for granted. When she was hired out to a family near Cambridge, Maryland, to do housework, she was tempted to taste one of the sugar cubes she saw in the sugar bowl. She popped one into her mouth – then was immediately convinced her mistress had seen her stealing. Fearing punishment, she ran away and hid in the pigsty. She stayed there for five days, eating what the pigs ate. This was not too great a hardship since in certain respects it was better than what she was normally given to eat. When she finally came out of hiding, she was whipped for running away.

Harriet was described as a willful and moody child – perhaps she was trying to express her independence. She was determined to do outdoor work, and Brodas finally gave in when she was nine years old and hired her out as a field hand. At least he would be able to get some money from her outdoor work instead of having other owners send her back all the time because she was a poor houseworker. Harriet did well in the fields. She enjoyed the outdoors, the feeling of almost being free since she was not being closely monitored. Outdoor work also had the side benefit of building up her strength and endurance, both of which would later serve her well. It also brought her into contact with slaves who travelled north with their masters and who told stories of possible escape routes and of the freedom that could be had by following the northerly flow of the Choptank River out of Maryland.

Harriet Tubman's Known Family

Benjamin and Araminta, father and mother. Both died in Auburn, New York in the 1870s.
John Henry (Ross) Stewart
William Henry (Ross) Stewart
Sophie Ross, sold further south
James Ross
Benjamin Ross
Moses Ross
Mary Ann
Robert Ross
Linah Ross, sold further south
Ann Marie (Ross) Stewart
Harriet

In comparison to other slaveholders, Harriet's owner may have been "fair," but he nonetheless showed little consideration for his slaves, particularly when he had financial problems. To raise money, he didn't hesitate to sell two of Harriet's older sisters, Linah and Sophie. This act not only separated the two girls from their parents and sisters and brothers, but also separated them from their own children. Unfortunately, this was all too common for slaves, and it was acts like this that made Harriet resolve to do everything she could to take control of her life and to someday make herself free.

The Turning Point

During fall evenings, field slaves worked as a group to clean up the wheat and husk the corn. One fall evening in 1835, Harriet saw a slave named Jim, from a neighbouring plantation, make a run for his freedom. Curious, Harriet ran along with his overseer, McCracken, who was chasing him. McCracken finally cornered Jim in the Bucktown General Store and demanded that

Harriet assist and tie up Jim. She refused to do this. Suddenly Jim bounded out the door, and Harriet blocked the doorway so that no one could catch him. McCracken responded to this by picking up an iron weight and throwing it. Perhaps he intended to hit Jim, but it hit Harriet in the forehead and nearly killed her. For months, in spite of everything Rit could do to help Harriet, she fell in and out of consciousness. After she seemed better, her owner tried to sell her, but because she had recurring bouts of sleeping attacks, sometimes as many as four a day, no one wanted her.

Called the "President of the Underground Railroad," Levi Coffin and his wife are portrayed assisting freedom seekers.

After she recovered sufficiently, Harriet went back to work in her owner's fields and was hired out to Dr. Thompson, who owned her father, commanding $50 dollars a week for her services. The custom was that a male slave could earn $100 to $150 a week for the same type of work as Harriet had to do. She drove oxen, carted and plowed when working at home, and she sometimes worked with her father. John Stewart, who was an overseer of her father, was a builder who also managed the Brodas estate. Stewart liked to brag about Harriet's strength, claiming that she could lift a full barrel or pull a plow just as well as an ox.

Although he was still a slave, Harriet's father, Ben, was now a timber inspector and supervised the cutting and hauling of timber for the Baltimore shipyards. When she was working with him, Harriet cut wood, split rails and hauled logs, producing half a cord of wood a day. Brodas now let Harriet keep a small portion of her earnings, which she used to buy a pair of oxen to help her in her work. It was unusual for a woman to be doing a man's job and even more unusual for a slave to buy and own anything. The Bucktown community surely would have been aware of this unique slave.

The sleeping seizures that had resulted from Harriet's head injury prevented her from being sold to Southern plantation owners who might not have been tolerant of her sleep attacks. They also kept her from being paired off to produce children, as did her plain appearance and small – 148 centimetre – frame. Harriet is reported to have looked as though she could not understand anything at times. She quickly learned to turn this dull, vacant look to her advantage, assuming this dullness around her master or overseer so that she could listen to them while seeming unaware of what was going on around her. Sometimes she even pretended to be having a sleep attack to learn more about her master's plans. In fact, many slaves came to know the plans of their owners as they would listen and watch them intently while seeming not to be aware at all.

One mind for the White man to see, another mind I know is me.

Manumission

By law, the captured Africans brought to the New World to be slaves were not considered to have status as a "person." Slaves were prevented by law from owning anything, and were regarded only in terms of the work they were expected to do. However, some slave owners through their last will and testament would grant freedom – manumission. This freedom might be given because of the loyalty of the slave; because the slave was too old to sell profitably; or even because of the owner's self-interest, such as fear of not getting into heaven for keeping enslaved persons.

Harriet was a very spiritual person, sharing with her parents, Ben and Rit, a strong faith in God. About the time of her head injury, she began having visions which guided her or gave her encouragement. She prayed about everything and took the meaning of her visions to be the response of God to her prayers. Recuperating also provided her with time to think through the impact of slavery on her life and how she could change her status.

Harriet replaced her work name of Araminta with her birth name, Harriet, when she was a teenager. In 1844, when she was about the age of 24, she married John Tubman, a freed Black man. John's surname resulted from his great-grandparents' bondage experience with the wealthy Tubman family of Dorchester County in Maryland. His parents had been manumitted, that is freed under the terms of Justice Richard Tubman's will. It was very unusual for a slave to marry a free person.

An Important Discovery

When Harriet learned from John how he gained his freedom, through his parents' manumission, she decided to have a lawyer check the will of Athon Pattison who had owned her grandmother, Modesty, before the Pattison family married into the Brodas family and brought their "property" with them. Modesty had come to the United States on a slave ship from Guinea and was sold to the Pattisons. Athon Pattison's will gave Modesty's daughter Rittia (Rit) to his granddaughter, Mary Pattison, the wife of Joseph Brodas.

" I give and bequeath unto my granddaughter, Mary Pattison," the will read, "one Negro girl called 'Rittia' and her increase until she and they arrive to 45 years of age." Through her investigation, Harriet discovered that her mother had been wrongfully kept in slavery and should have been free. As Rit's daughter she too was entitled to be free. However, instead of being manumitted, Rit was passed down to Mary and Joseph

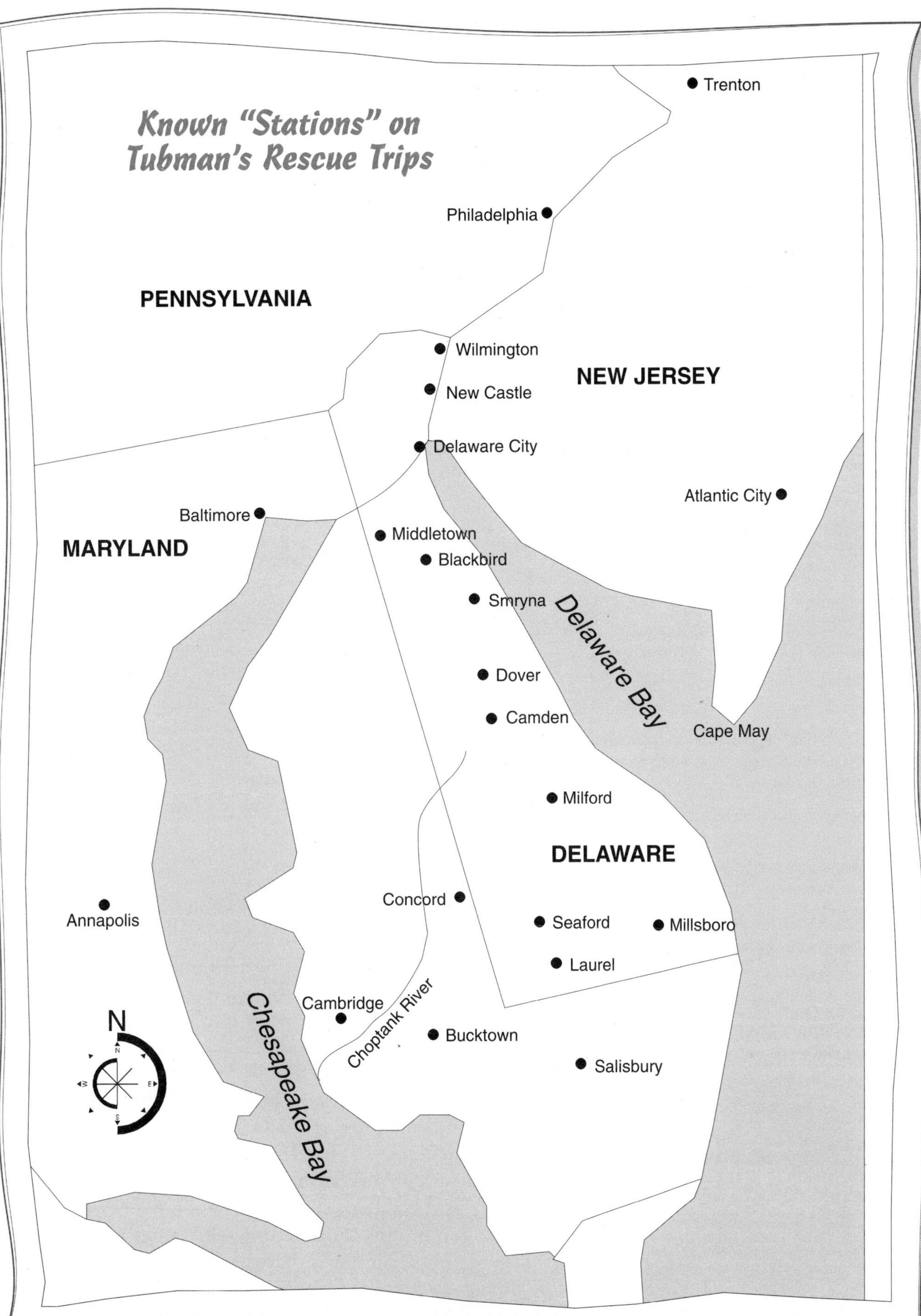
Known "Stations" on
Tubman's Rescue Trips
Trenton
Philadelphia
PENNSYLVANIA
Wilmington
New Castle
NEW JERSEY
Delaware City
Atlantic City
Baltimore
MARYLAND
Middletown
Blackbird
Smryna
Delaware Bay
Dover
Camden
Cape May
Milford
DELAWARE
Concord
Annapolis
Seaford
Millsboro
Laurel
Cambridge
Choptank River
Chesapeake Bay
Bucktown
Salisbury
N

Brodas's son Edward; instead of being free, Rittia and her children were still enslaved. This information deepened Harriet's resolve to be free and to see her family live in freedom.

The Moment of Decision

Early in 1849, Harriet heard that her master, Edward Brodas, planned to sell her and two of her brothers "in the chain gang to the far south" as soon as she recovered from one of her lengthy illnesses. Harriet did not want to be separated from her husband and family, and she did not want to be part of a southern cotton plantation. Not only was picking cotton back-breaking work but also in most places each slave's harvest was weighed at the end of the day and had to meet an expected quota. With her sleeping spells, she would surely fall behind in her harvesting duties and would be severely punished. Harriet would not survive long under those conditions – being sold south would be a certain death sentence for her, and she knew it.

For a long time, Harriet had been praying for "the dear Lord to change that man's [Edward Brodas] heart and make him a Christian," but she changed her prayer when she learned of his plans to sell her. She then began praying, "Lord, if you ain't never going to change that man's heart, kill him, Lord, and take him out of the way, so he won't do no more mischief." Edward Brodas died on March 7, 1849, after a lengthy illness. Harriet took his death as an answer to her prayer and it reinforced her faith. She and her brothers had been spared this time, but not for long.

Brodas had willed his possessions to his wife, Elizabeth, who was not interested in farming on her own, and Harriet was warned by another slave that she and her brothers were very soon to be sold further south. This news, combined with her recurring visions of lovely White ladies with welcoming outstretched arms waiting for her in the land of freedom, forced her to act. For Harriet there was only one choice: to be free. She should have been free, she desperately wanted to be free, and she felt now she had God's support. The time had come for her to seek her freedom.

Ever since she had learned that she should have been free, Harriet had hoped to persuade her husband to run away with her. But John Tubman was not interested in leaving. In fact, he even threatened to tell Harriet's owner of her plans to leave. The times they shared together after his refusal were very tense, as he watched her constantly to see if she would attempt to run. As much as she would have liked to

Marriages and Family Relationships

For enslaved Black people, there were no legal relationships only relationships that the master said were acceptable. A marriage depended on the whim of the master: If the master decided to sell the slaves, the married partners might not be sold together and they might even be forced to take new partners by their new masters. After one of the partners had been sold, it was not uncommon for one of the partners to have to travel over 100 miles to be with the family. And this would only be possible once a year.

Similarly, children of slave marriages or from forced unions between owners and slaves, might be sold away from their parents and family. Depending on the state and the year, children often took the same status as their mother: if she were a slave, the child was considered a slave.

To show commitment to each other, some practiced "jumping the Broom ceremony." Since they were prevented from having legal weddings, men and women who wished to live as a couple would jump over a broom as a symbol of their commitment to each other.

When enslaved people achieved their freedom, they were also free to legally marry and they often reaffirmed their marriage vows because of their religious convictions.

share her dream with him, she knew that she could not. She had to be on her guard at all times.

Initially, Harriet planned to flee with her two brothers. They actually set out for the North, but their overwhelming fear of recapture and punishment forced them to return. Fortunately their brief, nighttime absence had not been noticed. Two days later, Harriet set out on her own after alerting her niece Mary Ann of her intentions through the coded message in the lyrics of the hymn she sang.

When that old chariot comes
I'm going to leave you
I'm bound for the promised land
Friends, I'm going to leave you

I'm sorry friends, to leave you
Farewell! oh, farewell!
But I'll meet you in the mornin'
Farewell! oh, Farewell!

I'll meet you in the mornin'
When you reach the promised land;
On the other side of Jordan,
For I'm bound for the promised land.

From "A North-side View of Slavery"

Harriet Tubman's Story

I grew up like a neglected weed, ignorant of liberty, having no experience of it. Then I was not happy or contented: every time I saw a White man I was afraid of being carried away. I had two sisters carried away in a chain-gang – one of them left two children. We were always uneasy.

Now that I have been free, I know what a dreadful condition slavery is. I have seen hundreds of escaped slaves, but I never saw one who was willing to go back and be a slave. I have no opportunity to see my friends in my native land. We would rather stay in our native land, if we could be as free there as we are here. I think slavery is the next thing to hell. If a person would send another person into bondage, he would, it appears to me, be bad enough to send him into hell, if he could.

Mary Ann knew that Harriet was running, and as a worker being watched by the mistress in the big house, she was careful not to betray her. As soon as she was able, she alerted Harriet's parents, brothers and sisters. John Tubman would not have found out until later because he did not live on the plantation. Even married slaves, like Harriet, had to return to their master's plantation for the night after being hired out all day – marriage meant only that "spare" time (that is, Saturday night and Sunday, unless the master had other plans for your time) might be shared between husband and wife. When John realized that Harriet had gone, he advised her owner of Harriet's escape to find freedom in the North.

Chapter Three

Freedom from Slavery

When Harriet left, she took with her a home-made quilt admired by a Quaker woman that she had chanced to meet sometime before. This woman promised help should Harriet ever needed it. Harriet sought this woman and found her the day after her escape and traded the quilt for a piece of paper with two names on it, probably the names of other Quakers living farther north. She was told to sweep the yard until her contact's husband came home in the evening to avoid arousing the neighbours' suspicions.

Both the Quaker couple and Harriet had put themselves at risk. Since slaves were considered property, running away was viewed as stealing valuable property from the owner – a slave in search of freedom was committing a felony, stealing his or her future labour, and those who helped were assisting in the theft. If caught, a slave could be maimed, disfigured or killed as an example to others; those who helped could be harassed, isolated, fined or jailed – even, infrequently, severely beaten or killed.

Running away was not the sort of thing Black women usually did to resist slavery. It tended to be a man's form of resistance. Women might be held back by their desire to care for their children, or by the fact that they were closely supervised as they worked in the master's house and their absence would soon be noticed. To rebel against their enslavement, enslaved women might poison food, injure livestock, pretend to be ill, or even harm the children of the master. In other words, they used the means and opportunities that were possible in their situations. Running away required knowledge of where to go, physical stamina and outdoor survival skills, a combination that few women slaves had developed. Harriet was an exception. Her physical condition, aside from her sleeping seizures was excellent; she was strong. Her experiences working in the fields had equipped her with a knowledge of nature and survival skills that gave her confidence in her ability to succeed. Her strong religious convictions made her feel, like Joan of Arc, that she had God's support for her plans.

When the Quaker woman's husband arrived home, he drove Harriet, in a covered wagon, to the outskirts of another town. From there Harriet travelled on her own, following the winding Choptank River to Chesapeake Bay and the bay coast to Baltimore. It was a long, roundabout way to her ultimate destination – Philadelphia.

Harriet may have learned the safest route from other slaves, and she may have been given a ride out of Bucktown, but she had to rely on her own courage and initiative to leave the plantation and on her own wit and cunning to avoid recapture. Since she could not read or write, she had to plot her course by the North Star, called the "Drinking Gourd" by slaves, or by the moss growing on the north side of trees. She hid in the daytime, and even under cover of darkness, she avoided obvious routes, such as well-travelled roads, and tended to wade through swamps and rivers. "Running water," as she phrased it, "never tells no tales."

The magnificent interior of Mother Bethel African Methodist Episcopal Church in Philadelphia. While not identical to the church in which Tubman worshiped in the 1850s – since it has been rebuilt – the present church is erected on the oldest plot of land owned by people of African descent in the United States.

> There are two things I had a right to – liberty or death. If I could not have one, I would have the other: for no man should take me alive; I should fight for my liberty so long as my strength lasted. And when the time comes for me to go, the Lord would let them take me.

Harriet was intuitive and always seemed able to anticipate danger and to know whom she could approach for food and shelter. She herself always felt that a Divine presence assisted her in this and in finding strength to continue no matter how discouraged, hungry, tired, cold and wet she was.

Once Harriet reached the Camden, Delaware, area there would have been people to help her since that was the centre of Quaker abolitionist activity, and there were many free Black "conductors" to assist people along the Christiana River into Wilmington, Delaware. The Mason-Dixon Line, which separated the free states of the North from the slave states of the South, was just a short distance from Wilmington.

When Harriet had finally crossed over the "line," she was awestruck.

> "I looked at my hands to see if I was the same person now I was free. There was such a glory over everything, the sun came like gold through the trees, and over the fields, and I felt like I was in heaven."

Myths about the North

In the 1850s, Philadelphia was a booming metropolis and the centre of progressive social thought and action, and it had the largest population of free Blacks in the United States. Because of the supportive atmosphere Blacks found there, it was the favoured destination for freedom-seeking slaves escaping from the nearby slave-holding states.

White Southerners told enslaved people many exaggerated or false stories about life in the North to discourage them from trying to leave. Some said that all abolitionists spoke French and would make them worship idols or would boil them and eat them, or that nothing grows in the North except black-eyed peas. Others claimed that Blacks were executed there, or that rivers and lakes were thousands of miles wide, or that the climate was too cold and severe for a descendent of Africa. One freedom seeker, Lewis Clarke, reported after his determined escape that he was warned that he would have his head skinned, that Canadians would eat his children, poke their eyes out and have their hair made into coat collars. In spite of these dire warnings, enslaved Blacks fled north because they detested slavery and they realized these stories could not be true.

"Free" State

A "free" state was a state north of the Mason-Dixon line – the boundary between Pennsylvania and Maryland, the boundary between the northern, Union states, and the southern, Confederate states. In the free states, slave holding was not allowed by law. The free states came into being by 1777 and included Maine, Vermont, New Hampshire, New York and Pennsylvania. After the passage of the Fugitive Slave Act of 1850, these states were no longer safe for Blacks as they could be captured, tried and sent back to enslavement. As a result, Ontario, Quebec and the Maritimes in Canada became attractive for freedom seekers.

They knew because they were more intelligent than their masters usually gave them credit for. The house slaves paid attention to dinner-table talk about events off the plantation, and they listened to what slaves who had travelled north with their masters had to tell. These people had seen for themselves how Blacks lived free there. Sometimes they had been secretly advised by free Blacks that they could also achieve their freedom by crossing the river at a particular point, or by following the North Star just a little farther to Canada. If these educated slaves did not seek their freedom immediately because of concerns for their family still in bondage, they kept this information for future reference and passed on their knowledge to others.

By law, slaves were not allowed to learn how to read or write. Learning depended on what they could see or hear for themselves, or what they could pick up from others. Slaves would silently express their protest against the demands of slavery by pretending not to understand commands or by taking extra long to complete a task. To keep abreast of their master's business or social plans which would have an impact on the lives of the enslaved people on the plantation, the slaves would listen carefully while appearing to be disinterested. They would then pass this information on to others who might benefit from the information. Harriet Tubman is known to have had sleeping spells and often she would feign a spell to learn something without raising suspicions.

"One mind for the White man to see, another mind I know is me."

A New Beginning

In Philadelphia, Harriet lived with friends in a neighbourhood that was mainly Black. She worshipped at the nearby Mother Bethel African Methodist Church, which was built on the oldest plot of land continuously owned by African Americans in the United States, and supported herself by doing domestic work. She never stayed long in one job, partly so that no one would have the opportunity to identify her as a runaway and partly to experience the meaning of freedom and personal choice. Before long, however, Harriet began to feel lonely.

> "I had crossed the line [of freedom] of which I had so long been dreaming. I was free; but there was no one to welcome me to the land of freedom, I was a stranger in a strange land, and my home after all was down in the old cabin quarter, with the old folks, and my brothers and sisters. But to this solemn resolution I came: I was free, and they should be free also; I would make a home for them in the North, and the Lord helping me, I would bring them all there."

During the early part of 1850, Harriet saved all the money she earned from her positions as cook, seamstress, housekeeper, laundress and scrubwoman in the hotels and private homes of Philadelphia and Cape May, New Jersey. She was now ready to make her first attempt to free her family. She was also beginning to think of going back into slave-holding areas to free other slaves.

In order to stay informed about her relatives in the South, Harriet made contacts with free Black and White abolitionists who could read newspapers to find out about pending slave auctions and write coded letters to abolitionists in the South. This is how she learned that her niece Mary Ann now was living near Baltimore.

Harriet devised a plan to rescue Mary Ann. Because she didn't know how to write, she asked someone to write a letter to Mary Ann's husband, John Bowley, a free man. Harriet advised him that if he could get her to Baltimore she would conduct Mary Ann to Philadelphia. In December 1850, the rescue was almost thwarted when Mary Ann's master suddenly decided to sell her at an auction sale in Cambridge, Maryland. Harriet quickly developed an alternative plan that involved hiding Mary Ann in Cambridge even while the bidding on her was taking place and later spiriting her out of the area to freedom in a six-horse wagon. Harriet's first rescue was successful, and Mary Ann was later reunited with her husband and children.

Harriet may have borrowed passports, called "Freedoms," from the free Black residents of Philadelphia to assist her with Mary Ann's rescue and later ones. A "Freedom" was a passport that free Blacks were required to carry at all times to verify their free status to anyone who questioned it. She also may have identified government workers who were willing to look the other way and allow rescues to occur or who would accept bribes for their silence. As

From AME to BME

In 1794, while praying in church in Philadelphia, Reverend Richard Allen was pulled from his knees and commanded to go to the Black section of the church to pray. Following this, Reverend Allen founded the African Methodist Episcopal Church (AME). The Bethel AME church still stands on the oldest plot of land continuously owned by people of African descent in the United States.

This church was attended by Harriet Tubman while she was in Philadelphia. Many Black people coming into Canada brought their religion with them, but when the American Fugitive Slave Law was passed the people of African descent in Canada wanted to align themselves with the British since they were supported in British controlled Canada by law. Officially established in Chatham in 1856, branches of the British Methodist Episcopal Church of Canada BME were active across the country. Harriet Tubman is believed to have attended the branch of the BME that was across the street from where she lived, near the corner of North and Geneva. The BME is the oldest continuously functioning Black Canadian owned and operated church group in Canada.

well, Harriet began to develop a working relationship with a free Black abolitionist, William Still, who would have been able to assist her. Harriet formed an alliance with Thomas Garrett as well. Her success in freeing Mary Ann and her desire to see her family free, combined with her knowledge of who could help and how, soon prompted her to attempt another rescue.

Stockholders
of the Underground
R.R. Company
Hold on to Your Stock!!

The market has an upward tendency. By the express train which arrived this morning at 3 o'clock, fifteen thousand dollars worth of human merchandise, consisting of twenty-nine able-bodied men and women, fresh and sound, from the Carolina and Kentucky plantations, have arrived safe at the depot on the other side, where all our sympathising colonization friends may have an opportunity of expressing their sympathy by bringing forward donations of ploughs, etc., farming utensils, pick axes and hoes, and not old clothes; as these emigrants all can till the soil.
N.B. Stockholders don't forget the meeting to-day at 2 o'clock at the ferry on the Canada side. All persons desiring to take stock in this prosperous company, be sure to be on hand.

Detroit, April 19, 1853 By Order of the BOARD OF DIRECTORS[12]

Stockholders on the Underground Railroad donated their food, train passes, clothing or money to the work of freeing Blacks held in bondage.

This time Harriet targeted her brother John Ross and his sons, who were in Talbot County north of Dorchester County. John made it out with two other slaves, but he had to leave his sons behind because he had no way to separate them from their owner. Later, John Bowley, who had authentic freedom papers, was sent to free the boys. He was able to "kidnap" them in 1851 and return them to their self-emancipated father with the assistance of Harriet's planning and contacts.

About this time, Harriet attempted to bring her husband, John Tubman, to Philadelphia to join her. Even though he had not been supportive of her dream of also being free and had told her mistress that she had run away, Harriet still loved him. She was, therefore, bitterly disappointed to find that he had taken another wife (Caroline) and was hurt when they laughed at her suggestion that she conduct them north. Because of John's rejection, she became even more determined to find happiness in helping others. She decided that she would not be content until all of her people in bondage were free. So, in the fall of 1851, having heard of ten slaves who were interested in fleeing, Harriet went south to conduct them to freedom.

Harriet's experiences as a slave and an escapee proved useful in her numerous rescues. She knew that the best time to start out from the South with her passengers was Saturday night. Slaves did not have as rigid a routine on Sundays because their overseer had the day off, so their absence would not be immediately noticed. As well, handbills and newspaper notices alerting the community to the escape could not be printed until Monday because Christian printers closed their shops on Sunday. On her journeys, Harriet also made a point of travelling by night and resting by day to further avoid detection.

Harriet was deeply religious and felt that she was guided by a Divine presence. She declared that she heard mystical voices and she was convinced that "God had called her to lead her people out of bondage."

In spite of her successes and her dedication to freedom, there were times when "passengers" on Harriet's train doubted her ability to escort them north in safety. And who could blame them? It was not that easy to believe that this short, plain woman with sudden sleeping attacks could successfully get them to freedom. Harriet often tried to motivate her passengers and calm their fears by singing songs familiar to them, but when that was not enough she was known to pull out her pistol, or the equally lethal sharpened clam shells she carried, and threaten, "Live North or die here!" She later said of a passenger who wanted to return to his plantation and whom she had threatened into submission,

> "If he was weak enough to give out, he'd be weak enough to betray us all, and all who had helped us, and do you think I'd let so many die just for one coward man?"

Harriet Tubman was the leader on her freedom train, and she took her responsibility seriously.

A Rare Daytime Rescue

There was no physical difference between Blacks who were free and those who were slaves. Breeding of Africans by Europeans, produced slaves who were half African and half European, and over the generations they became increasingly less African-looking as the contact continued. Charles Nalle was a slave who was one-eighth Black, the child of a slave who was one-quarter Black and her White master. Nalle ran from his plantation in Culpepper County, Virginia, to join his wife. The agent who was sent to find him was his half brother – they had the same father, looked alike but one was a slave and one was free – and when he found him he had Charles Nalle arrested. Nalle was being held in the Commissioner's office when Harriet managed to grab him, while rousing the crowd outside the building, and put him into a waiting boat. On the other side of the river he was recaptured, freed by the crowd and Harriet was able to arrange a ride to safety for him on a passing wagon. Nalle later returned with money collected from the community to buy his freedom.

All the way to Canada

By the end of 1850, after passage of the Fugitive Slave Act, the northern states were no longer a safe place for freedom-seeking slaves – or even for Blacks who were legally free. This Act, which took effect in 1851, stipulated that any Black person accused by a White person of being a runaway could be arrested anywhere in the United States. Moreover, once charged, Black people could not testify on their own behalf or be represented by a lawyer. In the eyes of the law, if you were Black, then you were likely an escaping slave who ought to be captured. As a Black, if you had achieved some measure of wealth through hard work, your business, home or other assets might seem attractive to someone who would then accuse you of being an escaped slave.

The Act also stated that any person aiding a runaway slave could be fined $1000 or face six months in jail. To make matters worse, the special Commissioners who chaired the hearings were paid on the basis of their verdicts. They received twice as much money for every Black person they sent back to the South and perpetual slavery as they got for those who went

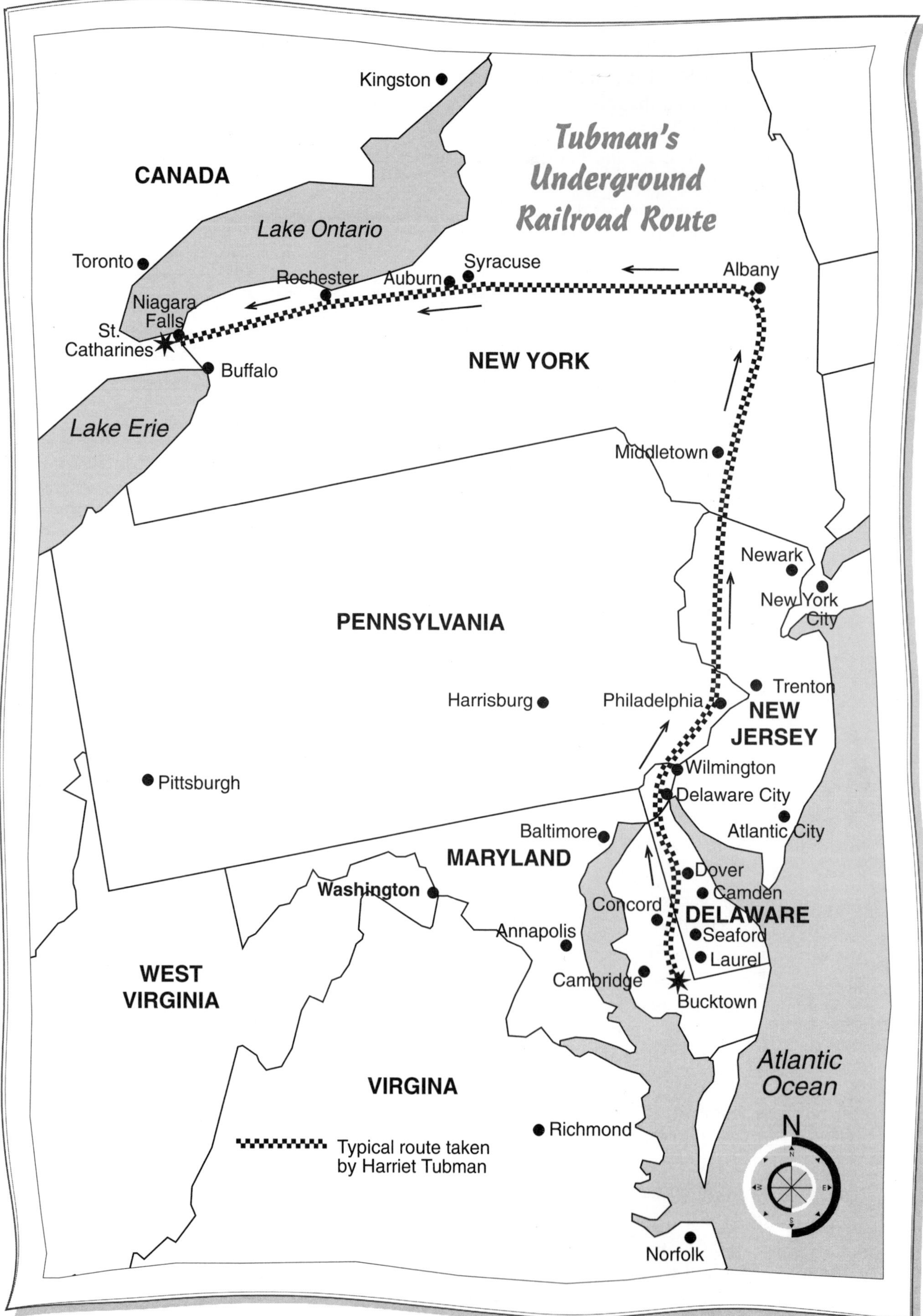
Tubman's Underground Railroad Route
Kingston
CANADA
Lake Ontario
Toronto
Rochester
Auburn
Syracuse
Albany
Niagara Falls
St. Catharines
Buffalo
NEW YORK
Lake Erie
Middletown
Newark
New York City
PENNSYLVANIA
Harrisburg
Philadelphia
Trenton
NEW JERSEY
Pittsburgh
Wilmington
Delaware City
Baltimore
Atlantic City
MARYLAND
Dover
Washington
Camden
Concord
DELAWARE
Annapolis
Seaford
Laurel
WEST VIRGINIA
Cambridge
Bucktown
Atlantic Ocean
VIRGINA
Richmond
N
Typical route taken by Harriet Tubman
Norfolk

free. It was, therefore, more profitable for them to support enslavement. Suddenly, the legal and social system which had provided some measure of support for free Blacks was being used against them.

Harriet, her passengers and her family were now at terrible risk, so she looked to a country that presented itself as the most accessible refuge in which to find freedom: Canada.

The Appeal of Canada

By 1850, there were about ten thousand Blacks living in Canada, mainly in southern Ontario and Nova Scotia. Some were descendants of enslaved or free Africans who had come or been brought to Canada generations before. More, however, were the descendants of Black Loyalists who had been promised freedom and assistance if they fought for the British during the American War of Independence around 1783. Many others had supported the British during the War of 1812 in return for similar promises, while still others were escaped slaves who had sought refuge in Canada after slavery was abolished throughout the British Empire, including Canada, in 1834.

Canada was thus widely seen by American Blacks as a place where their rights and privileges would be protected. It had other attractions as well: it was close enough to be reached by land; in Ontario, it was English speaking; the climate was similar to that of the northern United States; and there were opportunities to become self-supporting.

By the time Harriet decided to make her fourth rescue to get her brother James, his wife and children and nine others, she had also decided that the final destination for them would be Canada. This, of course, made the trip longer and more dangerous, but again Harriet was successful. In December 1851, she and 11 fugitives arrived safely in St. Catharines, Ontario – her first rescue mission to Canada.

The Journey of Harriet Tubman

"She used a variety of routes…[but] usually she followed the lone trail that led from Cambridge over the Choptank River bridge to the Delaware towns of Camden, Dover, Smyrna and Odessa, to Wilmington, where her close friend, Thomas Garret, was always waiting with food and funds. From this friendly home she led the way through southern Chester County, Pennsylvania, into Philadelphia before continuing her dangerous journey into upstate New York and finally across the suspension bridge of Niagara Falls into Canada."

Charles Blockson

Chapter Four

St. Catharines, Her Home in the 1850s

Even before the first Loyalist arrivals, Black people were a part of the settlement of Ontario. At first, there were only a few settlers, but over the years a small but steady stream of Black Loyalists and many escaped slaves arrived to swell their numbers. They settled throughout southern Ontario, some in predominantly Black communities such as the Dawn, Elgin and Wilberforce settlements, others scattered among the rest of the population in villages, towns and cities.

St. Catharines, Ontario, is located on the south shore of Lake Ontario, about 20 kilometres from the Niagara River, which forms the border between Canada and the United States. The area, known as the Niagara Peninsula, enjoys many natural advantages that made it attractive to settlers in the late eighteenth and early nineteenth centuries. Foremost among these are a mild climate that allows orchards and gardens to thrive, and an abundance of the fresh water required for farming, transportation of goods and power to operate mills. There were also many mineral springs thought to have medicinal qualities.

As in the rest of southern Ontario, permanent, English, non-Native settlement around St. Catharines began in the 1780s, when many United Empire Loyalists – Americans who had chosen to remain loyal to Britain during the American Revolution – were drawn to the area. The first settlements were mainly agricultural, and since this was some of the best farmland in the country, the people prospered. Real boom times, however, came to the area in the 1820s with the building of the Welland Canal. Opened in 1829, the canal created a navigable waterway between Lake Erie and Lake Ontario. This not only allowed faster and easier transportation of local produce and other goods, but also the water power produced at every lock led to the development of major industries, including mills, shipyards and metal manufacturers.

All this development created jobs – jobs in the new factories and mills; jobs producing, transporting and selling food and everything else needed by a growing population; jobs in the canal itself since work to improve it continued almost nonstop for decades. About the same time, the opportunities presented by the mineral springs became recognized. Hotels and other facilities were built, and before long St. Catharines was attracting large numbers of American tourists who came to benefit from the healthful waters.

By the 1850s, St. Catharines was well known as one of the terminals of the Underground Railroad and had a resident African-Canadian population of over a thousand out of a total population of about 7000. It also had several organizations devoted to helping incoming escapees. The most prominent was the Refugee Slaves' Friends Society (RSFS) formed in 1852. William Hamilton Merritt, the local businessman who had organized the building of the Welland Canal, was a member of the RSFS, and the first mayor of St. Catharines. This organization offered financial, employment and housing assistance to fugitives, and worked to send some of the now-free Blacks to Toronto.

St. Catharines' Black Community

Most of the Black residents of St. Catharines, whether American– or Canadian-born, were self-supporting. The majority worked as labourers on the canal or in the town's mills, foundries, factories and machine shops. Some, however, were skilled trades people, including masons, coopers, barbers, or carpenters. Others, men and women, were employed in the homes of wealthier Whites as cooks and housekeepers; still others had farms nearby. One visitor to the area at the time noted,

> Scattered around, and within five miles [eight km] are large numbers of [Black] farmers, many of whom have become wealthy since escaping into Canada. Going into the market on Saturday morning, I counted 37 coloured persons selling their commodities, consisting of ducks, chickens,

William Hamilton Merritt, MP

Born in Bedford, West Chester County, New York, on July 3, 1793, Merritt's father was a United Empire Loyalist and a military man who served with a unit commanded by Colonel John Graves Simcoe. Upon learning of Simcoe's new appointment as Lieutenant Governor of Upper Canada (now, Ontario), he visited his old friend in Niagara and moved his family to Canada when William was three years old. Merritt's father was appointed sheriff of the Niagara district and purchased land on Twelve Mile Creek and the area became known as Merriton. His father was also credited with promoting the healthful qualities of the springs in St. Catharines.

As a young man, William Merritt fought in the War of 1812 and following the war he opened a general store, sawmill and flour mill on the site of present-day St. Catharines, besides purchasing some three hundred acres (120 hectares) of land nearby. He promoted the transportation system to enhance commerce between Ontario and New York State, including construction of the Welland Canal, which saw the first boats through the canal on October 24, 1829.

By 1832 he was elected to the legislature of Upper Canada and continued his interest in transportation facilities between the two countries. In the 1840s he developed the concept of the Niagara Suspension Bridge, which was completed by 1849 and used by escaping slaves in the following years. He died on July 5, 1864.

> eggs, butter, cheese, hams, bacon, vegetables and fruits of all kind.

People of African descent were highly motivated to be "industrious," to be hard working and to live morally. Abolitionists supported temperance as a way of encouraging good work habits and harmonious relations with others. The African Temperance Society of St. Catharines was formed by local Blacks to ensure that former slaves now in Canada would continue to demonstrate that they could take care of themselves and take advantage of opportunities now that they were free.

In the early 1840s Blacks were also asked to patrol the Welland Canal to keep the peace between Catholic and Protestant workers of Irish background. The security role for Blacks was an extension of their military service in the Colored Corps during the War of 1812 and the Rebellion of 1837 in Upper Canada. Before the Colored Corps was disbanded in 1851, it also played a role in anti-smuggling efforts and on road construction.

On my Underground Railroad, I never ran my train off the track and I never lost a passenger.

Wherever they settled, Blacks tended to live close to each other because they faced similar economic problems and social barriers. Their homes were usually located on the outskirts of town, on land that was not considered desirable at the time. Because they lived close together, churches and schools grew to meet their needs as a community. In St. Catharines, the Black community lived primarily in the area bounded by North, Geneva, Welland and Williams streets. Oliver Phelps and William Hamilton Merritt owned a large tract of land in this area, which they had made available to Black people at reasonable rates. It seems that in some cases Black residents were not charged interest and may even have been forgiven some payments if they were unable to manage the expense. Some sources suggest Merritt donated a lot of land for the building of a church and meeting hall for the Black community along the North Street area. Land for the BME Church was purchased by the Black community, and assistance in building the church came from the members of St. Paul Street Methodist Church, a non-Black congregation. These cooperative relations exist to this day.

The Black community of St. Catharines was viewed in a positive light. According to Mary Ann Shadd, the first Black woman newspaper publisher in North America:

> "During my stay at St. Catharines I had frequent opportunities of examining the general improvements of the

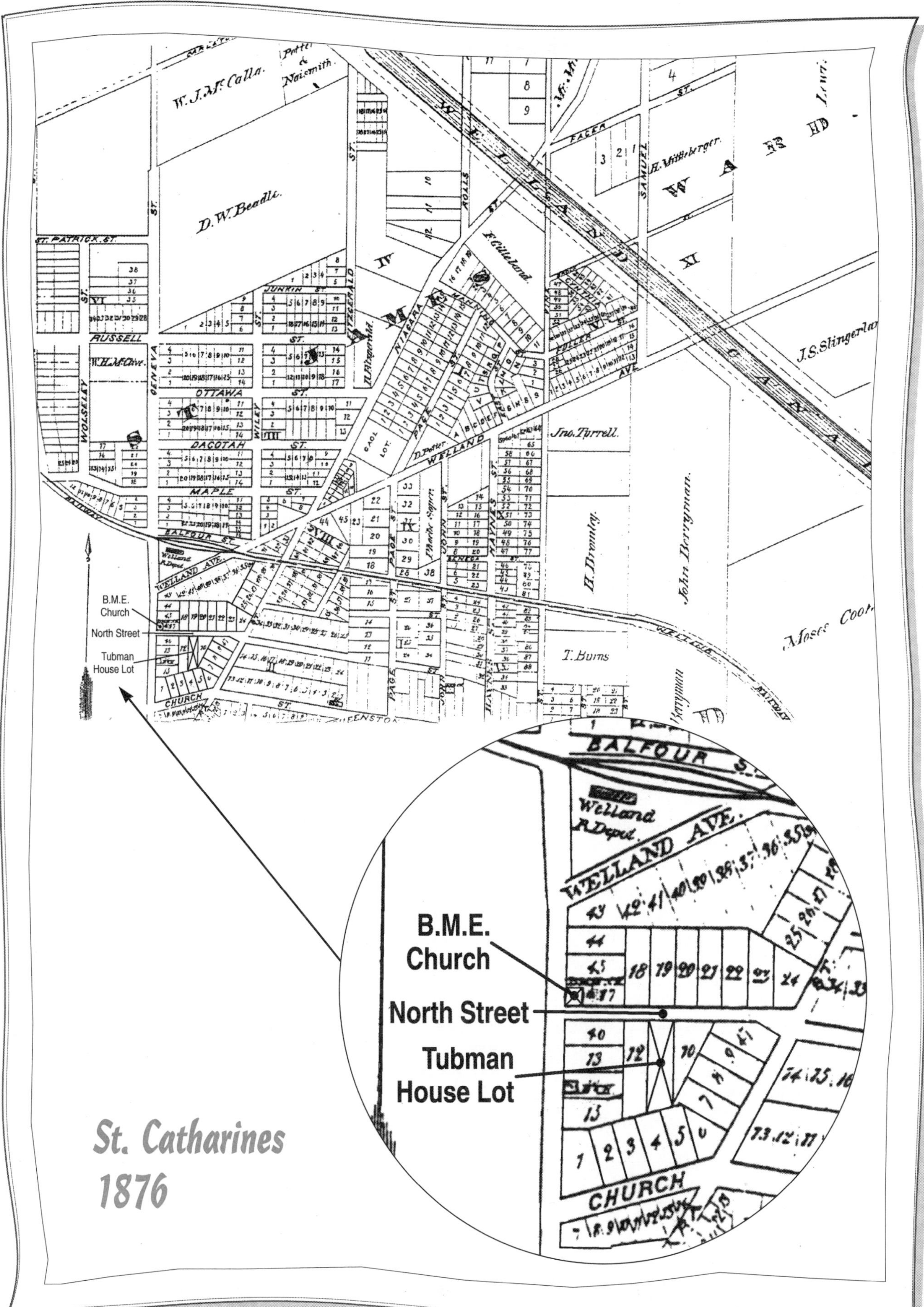
B.M.E. Church
North Street
Tubman House Lot
WELLAND AVE.
BALFOUR ST.
CHURCH
Welland R.Depot
D. W. Beadle
W. J. McCalla
J.S. Slingerland
Jno. Terrell
John Berryman
H. Bromley
T. Burns
RUSSELL
OTTAWA
DACOTAH
MAPLE
JUNKIN ST.
ST. PATRICK ST.
WOLSELEY
GENEVA
WILLEY
NIAGARA
PAGE ST.
JOHN ST.
HAYNES ST.
SAMUEL
GAOL LOT
St. Catharines
1876

place and was in no way more gratified than when viewing the snug homesteads of the coloured people. Messrs. Maddern, Young, Lindsay and others are adding largely by their enterprise to the beauty of the place. Their success is a standing refutation to the falsehood that begging is needed for the fugitives of St. Catharines."

Reverend Ward's Letter to the Editor of *The Globe*, **Regarding the Riots in St. Catharines**:

Mr. Editor,
Your well-known impartiality and justice to all parties, as a journalist, embolden me to hand you the following account of the riot in the St. Catharines difficulties. You will see the matter differs somewhat from the published accounts of it. I have the facts from a reliable source (a gentleman who was an eye witness) of undoubted veracity.

After the Militia drill, the Colonel spoke in terms of commendation and encouragement of the Black corps, whereupon several of the White soldiers began to throw the most disgusting and filthy substances upon the Blacks. The latter appealed to Captain Clark for protection against this outrage. Captain C. promptly rebuked the Whites, who for a while obeyed his orders. Subsequent to this, a Black man, named Harris, was sitting upon a fence, near the parade ground; a White man, without provocation, knocked Harris from the fence with a stone. Harris went to several Justices of the Peace for redress, but sought justice from them in vain. He then, in the heat of passion, repaired to Stinson's tavern, where this White man was, and flogged him. Thence arose the general melee. Upon the request of several leading White persons, the Blacks gave up the clubs with which they were defending themselves against superior numbers of Whites, while the latter continued their assault upon the former. Then the Blacks resorted to stones, with which they fought, until the Whites were reinforced by the fire brigade.

The damage done to the property of the Blacks was done by the firemen alone.

The difficulty was finally adjusted by the Whites agreeing to repair all damages done to the property of the Blacks, which they have promptly and honourably done.

It is gratifying to know that the riot did not commence with the Blacks, that the officers of the regiment behave impartially, that the Blacks resorted to no violence until provoked beyond endurance, that they gave up their weapons when requested to do so; and that so just and honourable a settlement of the matter was made. May it prove to be a "finality!" Your obedient servant,

Rev. S. R. Ward

Concerns About St. Catharines

After the Fugitive Slave Act of 1850 was passed, the small stream of Blacks fleeing oppression in the United States became a flood. The first smaller wave of Black settlers had been reasonably well accepted because of the need for workers. Now, however, concerns about Canada's relations with the United States, prejudices about people of African descent, and the challenge of absorbing so many new immigrants contributed to incidents between Black and non-Black St. Catharines residents.

While Black Canadians had helped build at least one of the resort spas, the Welland House, they were denied service at this hotel because of their colour. It was felt that it might offend the White American tourists. In one case, a Black minister and his wife travelling to Buffalo were refused accommodation during a blinding snowstorm.

In 1852, a group of Black military men who were parading were attacked without provocation by a group of young White people who then went on to damage or destroy homes in the African-Canadian community. The attackers' reason: outrage at the sight of Black men parading in British uniform. To its credit, the town of St. Catharines voted in 1853 to pay for the damages to the Black settlement caused by this riot.

In 1854, Blacks were outraged that the public transportation, run by two hotels, the St. Catharines House and the American Hotel, would not carry them. When two Black ministers of the AME Church

The Welland House was built by African Canadians and supplied jobs for them in the 1800s. The Welland House and the other spa hotels (The Springbank and Stephenson House) developed around the local salt springs which were thought to have healing powers. Attracted by these springs, affluent people from around the world, especially the United States, flocked to St. Catharines for rest and relaxation. Guests of the spas included Mary Todd Lincoln – the widow of Abraham Lincoln – the aunt of Robert E. Lee, various spies, and tourists from the American South who travelled with their enslaved Black staff. Because the White guests from the South expected that Blacks in St. Catharines would be subservient, they forced the hotel owners to exclude Blacks from equal access in the hotels, giving rise to racial conflict. Today, the spas are closed and only the structure of the Welland House remains.

were among those denied transportation, a meeting was called at the British Methodist Episcopal Church. A plan of action was developed by these ministers, some waiters of the hotels and some other residents. After the head waiter of the American Hotel threatened to quit his job in protest and was supported by a St. Catharines House waiter, a list of resolutions was drawn up that included the following:

> **Resolved**, That in this glorious land of Freedom, and under this equitable and powerful Government, man is man, without respect to the colour of his skin, and that we, as men, will not submit to degrading terms of

> service, nor see our brethren treated with indignity by public conveyances, or excluded therefrom, without showing a manly spirit of resentment.
>
> **Resolved**, That, as waiters, at the public hotels, of St. Catharines, we will not continue in the service of our present employers, unless, in the management of their conveyances, they henceforth treat ourselves and our people with the respect and civility, to which we are entitled, as men.

A "refugee's" comment about St. Catharines:

"Refuge! Refuge for the oppressed!

Refuge for Americans escaping from abuse and cruel bondage in their native land!....

Refuge and rest!"

With this expression of affirmation and solidarity and with the support of influential members of the community who threatened to boycott these establishments, the hotels changed their policies to treat Blacks equally.

The frequency of such incidents multiplied as the decade wore on. With increased European immigration to Canada, the interest in tolerating or supporting people of African descent was waning, and it continued to do so even after the 1863 abolition of slavery in part of the United States ended the influx of African Americans. Many people seemed to feel that the Blacks could go home to the United States, or at the very least, back where they had come from – some place else. It was a time of White encouragement for Black people to resettle in the Caribbean Islands, Africa or remote outposts as if their usefulness had been outlived, as if they were not rooted to the soil they had tilled.

Education

In 1850, the Common Schools Act in Canada West allowed for the creation of separate schools for Blacks or Catholics, schools apart from those attended by most White Christians. While Blacks wanted to send their children to the best equipped or the nearest schools, White residents in many places protested the presence of Black children in public schools and were able to use the Act to create separate institutions for them.

Advertisements in the St. Catharines *Standard* required teachers with at least a third-class standing qualification for the Coloured School, established in 1856, while White students would be taught by teachers with no less than second or first class standing. In general, Blacks were opposed to such segregation as they felt such a policy would separate them from society and limit their children's future opportunities. Black parents in St. Catharines later used the power of the vote to defeat the election of a school trustee who was considered to be supportive of segregated schools. Protests continued until 1873 at which time the St. Catharines Committee on School Management reported that "mixing coloured and White children in the same classes would prove destructive to the efficiency of the school."

Schools in St. Catharines were later integrated despite the concerns of a few about the effects of social contact between the races.

An Underground Railroad Escape Story: The Story of Lucy Canada and Stephen Street

The following account is told by their daughter Henrietta Street:

"My mother, Lucy Canada, was born in Parkers Burgh, West Virginia, in 1813. Her father's name was Arion Keneday and her mother's name was Milla Canada. Her mother had two brothers, William and George, and one sister, Melinda. They were owned by Barnes Beckwith. Lucy's mother often said that they were not treated like slaves, but she could not bear the thought of not belonging to herself, and especially the thought that her three children were not free.

My father, Stepney Street, belonged to another man, Billy Neil, and his home was about 7 miles [4 km] from where mother lived. Father learned that his master was about to sell him and father decided to run away, travelling under the name of Frank Hammond. After the trials of hiding and travelling, father finally arrived in Windsor in Canada. About six weeks later, mother and three of her children followed him, along with her brothers and a fellow servant named Mero Bansom, whose complexion was so white that he could openly seek aid while the others hid nearby. The group finally arrived at Astibula, New York. There they boarded a schooner and landed at Point Albino, Ontario, and moved on to the nearby town of Bertie. When they were settled, mother advertised to find her husband who heard about their escape and that the family had arrived in Canada. He soon joined the family. We then moved to St. Catharines to a farm owned by Peter Smith. There the family was converted to the Zion Church and attended that church in St. Catharines.

Eventually, they settled on the Grand River. Here, they found the same God that had brought us from the land of bondage and in that humble cabin they erected an altar to the Almighty God. God to whom they served with four others (John Taylor, Rosanne Allan, Robert Bailey and Kisie Allan). Then at the age of 19, mother married father who was 26 years old."

[*Harriet Tubman is known to have assisted the family in their escape to freedom.*]

Chapter Five

Harriet's Years in St. Catharines

Why did Harriet Tubman choose St. Catharines over other possible safe destinations as her Canadian base? Because Harriet had to keep much of her activities a secret so that she would not be caught, she may have come to Canada before her December 1851 rescue, established contact with persons involved with the Underground Railroad to ensure the safety of her "passengers," and rented a house to which she could bring them. She must have been aware of the racist stirrings that made St. Catharines a less than ideal place for Black people to start a new life.

Perhaps, since she was still relatively fresh from her plantation experiences, Harriet found more positive than negative aspects in the St. Catharines community. Certainly, it's distance from the American border suited her. It was inland just enough not to be attractive to bounty hunters who might cross the border into Canada in search of escaped slaves, but close enough to the border to mean that her Underground Railroad trips were fairly short. As well, the industrial growth in the area ensured that former enslaved Africans would be able to support themselves. Another reason may have been that Harriet liked to have a main contact in each town she passed through, someone whom she felt she could trust completely, someone who could provide unconditional support to herself and her people. In St. Catharines, Reverend Hiram Wilson provided such support.

Hiram Wilson was born in New Hampshire and had settled in Toronto after completing his religious studies. Acting as an agent for the American Anti-Slavery Society, he travelled throughout Ontario and established ten schools. He worked with Josiah Henson to establish the British North America Institute in Dresden, Ontario. In 1850, however, he was saddened by the death of his wife and concerns over the financial management of the Dresden scheme. He was about to return to the United States when the passing of the Fugitive Slave Act changed his mind, and he decided to remain in Canada to assist the large numbers of fugitives entering the country. He chose to settle in St. Catharines, where he operated a fugitive relief station with financial support from the American Missionary Association. Wilson would later represent St. Catharines at the North American Convention of Free Colored Men as one of the four White delegates in Toronto. At the convention, it was decided that

Canada was the preferred destination for freedom seekers. Working with Wilson was Jermaine Loguen, an ordained AME Zion minister who had come to St. Catharines to avoid being arrested in Syracuse, New York, for his part in helping a slave escape. A self-freed man himself, Loguen worked not only with the church but also with the Underground Railroad movement in New York State. His own experiences and his expertise with fugitives made him a helpful addition to the abolition group in St. Catharines.

The house Harriet rented was in the Black district of St. Catharines, close to the British Methodist Episcopal Church of Canada (BME) on Geneva Street. Harriet worshipped at this church, which still serves the present-day community.

Considering the need for the secrecy of her missions to the South to rescue enslaved Blacks trying to escape, it is understandable that there are few records of Harriet's life in St. Catharines. It is likely that she supported herself there in much the same way as she had in Philadelphia or Cape May. She probably worked as a housekeeper, cook or laundress, which would be in keeping with the types of jobs that other Black women would have had. Service positions were occupations that many Blacks and lower class Whites had to do; only a few were able to break into businesses of their own. These were people seeking to survive, and any respectable means of earning money for their survival would be acceptable. These were also the types of jobs that would allow Harriet the flexibility to leave whenever she wished, making it easy to leave a job to carry out rescue missions in the South. Harriet never asked for anything for herself, but if her wages did not supply her with enough money for the care of the many fugitives, or self-emancipated people, she had living with her, she might have turned to others for assistance.

During Harriet's first winter in St. Catharines, we are told, she and her group "earned their bread" by chopping wood in the snows of a Canadian forest, even though frost-bitten, hungry and naked. Harriet was their good angel. She kept house for her brother, and the poor creatures boarded with her. She worked for them, begged for them and carried them by the help of God through the hard winter."

The North American Convention

Beginning in the 1830s, free Black people and other abolitionists often met at conventions. Initially, these gatherings allowed people to share their concerns and to plan ways to end slavery. Interested Black people would invite others to their city to have these meetings.

One of the most important of these meetings was the North American Convention held in the St. Lawrence Hall in Toronto on September 11–13, 1851. It started a trend of discussing Black nationalism and emigration of slaves to Canada. Called by many Ontario Blacks, such as Henry Bibb, editor of the *Voice of the Fugitive*, and James Theodore Holly, an American free-born Black who was devoted to emigration, the convention concluded with the agreement that Canada was a preferred destination for freedom seekers. Other options, such as the West Indies or Africa, were too far from Black abolitionist centres. Canada was a more convenient location from which to initiate the escapes of slaves or to assist in the establishing of African-Canadian settlements. Canada, in the eyes of the Black community, was considered to be a "beacon of hope" to the enslaved.

The historic Salem Chapel of the BME Church in St. Catharines. The BME Church is the oldest continuous Canadian Black owned and operated church in Canada. This building was constructed in a style similar to southern Black churches and some of the logs used in its construction can still be seen inside the church. Tubman lived next door to the church and worshiped here.

Harriet quickly developed a wide network of Underground Railroad contacts in Canada and the United States. In St. Catharines she was an active member of the interracial Refugee Slaves Friends Society (RSFS), and she was later on the executive of the Fugitive Aid Society (FAS). Across the border in the United States, she worked with several of the most prominent American abolitionists, including Frederick Douglass, William Still and Thomas Garrett. Frederick Douglass, orator and a self-emancipated man, gave freedom seekers shelter in his home in Rochester, New York. William Still kept records of Blacks who needed assistance in order to unite families, including his own, in Philadelphia. Thomas Garrett routinely escorted passengers across the Christiana River. Both Still and Garrett documented Harriet's work, indicating that she made at least eight trips between 1851 and 1856. Harriet later claimed to have made nineteen or more trips before the Civil War, eleven of these probably beginning and ending in St. Catharines.

How Adam Nicholson Came to St. Catharines,

"...The [escape] stories do say, however that Adam Nicholson, (Noreen) Smith's grandfather, swam to Canada and freedom that day in the mid 1800s. A burlap sack was the only clothing on the fugitive's scarred back.

Nicholson was already familiar with St. Catharines, having travelled there as a slave when his owner visited the city's popular mineral baths. When his former master tried to reclaim him on a later sojourn at the Welland House Hotel, he was not afraid to stand his ground in his new home and declare himself free."

From "What's Up Niagara", Oct. 12, 1993

Harriet made St. Catharines the base of her Underground Railroad work. From St. Catharines she launched her rescue missions into the United States and her visits to other known Black settlements in Ontario. She likely moved around Ontario to observe how her charges were managing in their freedom, and to determine where her future passengers might settle, as well as to investigate potential allies in her cause.

Organizations Helping the New Canadians

William Hamilton Merritt, called the "Father of Canadian Transportation" for his work with the Welland Canal, was a member of the Refugee Slaves' Friends Society (RSFS) formed in 1852. This organization offered financial, employment and housing assistance to fugitives, and many local Blacks, including Harriet Tubman were involved with it. The first Mayor of St. Catharines, Elias Smith Adams, was a founder of RSFS. In addition to providing immediate relief to "fugitives," the RSFS worked to send the now-free Blacks to Toronto. As reflected in the 1861 census, many of the surnames of African Canadians who settled for a time in St. Catharines continue among contemporary Blacks in the Toronto area. Names like Ball, Hollingsworth, Miles and Jackson exist among Toronto families which have long roots in Canada. Other families documented in the 1861 census, such as Jones, Miller, Sheffield and Stewart, have descendants living in St. Catharines, Hamilton, Brantford, Cayuga, Collingwood, Owen Sound, Windsor and London.

Mayor Elias Smith Adams

Born in the Twelve Mile Creek district in 1800, Adams's father had built the first tavern in the area. Elias Adams served as a member of the town council and became the mayor of the Town of St. Catharines in 1852. He was an abolitionist and a founder of the Refugee Slaves' Friends Society. Along with Merritt and others, Adams did what he could to support the growing Black population who were arriving in the area without food or shelter. He retired from politics in 1859, and died soon afterward.

ASSESSMENT ROLL FOR THE

NAMES OF TAXABLE PARTIES. | VALUE AND DESCRIPTION OF

	2	3	4	5	6	7	8	9	10	11	12	13
	OCCUPANTS.	PROFESSION, OCCUPATION, &c.	Free-holders.	House-holders.	Age.	OWNERS AND ADDRESS.	Non-Resident.	School Section.	Street, Square, or other designation.	No. of Lot or House, &c.	No. of Acres, Feet or other Measurement.	Value of each Lot.
											135½	$0700
59	Tenderling Theadore	Painter		1	26	E.S. Frieman			Church St			
	Tubman Harriet Col'd			1		Joseph Robinson			North "			
79	Thomas Alexander	Blk Smith	1		44				Geneva "			
74	Turner Jacob		1				1					5000
71	Tresly James	Carpenter		1	24	Samuel St John			Church St			
120	Tracey Cornelius	Teamster		1	26	Gershom Wright			Queenston "			
153	Tinline William	Ship Carpenter		1	25	Elizabeth Kelly			" "			
105	Tommy Wm.	Widow	1						Division "			
121	Taylor Richard	Miller	1		54				Queenston "			
202	Tacker Walther	Machinist	1		26				Page Plot			
419	Turnbull Lock John	Lock Master							Canal			
170	Tuite Thomas	Laborer		1	60	Wm A Merritt			North Patch			
283	Timmons Patrick	"		1					" "			
302	Towers Loisa	Widow										
	Underwood Richard Col'd	Laborer		1		E.M. Carroll			Queenston			

From the Assessment Roll, we learn that Harriet Tubman rented her St. Catharine's home. Notice the "Col'd" after her name, an abbreviation of "Coloured."

Harriet was one of the Blacks who was an active member of the inter-racial RSFS and she was on the executive of the Fugitive Aid Society (FAS) in 1861. She is credited with being the reason for the success of the FAS. Harriet's work in conducting people from the land of bondage to the land of freedom contributed to the importance of St. Catharines with the Underground Railroad. She was obviously interested in making sure that all of "her people" would get the assistance they would need when they reached their new home.

In the midst of her rescue work, Harriet never forgot the members of her family who remained in the South. In 1854, she felt that something was wrong in Bucktown, and this was confirmed through Underground Railroad communication. Someone who was secretly working with the Underground Railroad passed a message on to someone who passed it on to someone else until it finally reached Harriet. In this way, Harriet learned that her brothers Benjamin, Henry, and Robert were to be sold on December 26. She decided to send a coded letter to a free Black man named Jacob Jackson who could read and who knew her family. But he was under suspicion of helping slaves escape, and so to protect all concerned, Harriet had to find an indirect method of communicating her intentions. She solved the problem by having the letter "signed" by Jacob

Jackson's adopted free son, who lived in the North. The letter was received by Jackson, but not until it had been first read by his employer – even free Blacks could not expect privacy or respect for their mail – who did not understand its meaning, although he consulted others in the community about it. The letter said in part,

> Read my letter to the old folks, and give my love to them, and tell my brothers to be always watching unto prayer, and when the good ship of Zion comes along, to be ready to step on board.

Jackson, having no parents or brothers, pretended he did not understand it when questioned by his White overseer, but he immediately told Harriet's brothers to get ready because Harriet was coming to get them. On Christmas Eve, just two days before they were to be sold, Harriet met her brothers near their parent's cabin. With them were three other freedom seekers: John Chase, Peter Jackson and Jane Kane. Harriet's brothers knew that they would not expect Harriet's mother, Rit, to be quiet if she knew that Harriet was there. She would be too excited! However, they did let Ben know that they were leaving and he discreetly brought food to the group as they hid during the day. He covered his eyes with a bandanna so that he could truthfully be able to say, when questioned by his owner as he knew he would be, that he had not "seen" his sons. The group made good their escape and after travelling the 160 kilometres to Wilmington, Delaware, the fugitives were assisted by Thomas Garrett. They finally arrived in St. Catharines in early 1855.

Anthony Burns

Born a slave in Virginia on May 31, 1834, Burns was owned by Colonel Charles Suttle. He was hired out to work for others by Suttle and was able to escape and finally ended up in Boston. On May 24, 1854, he was arrested in Boston under terms of the Fugitive Slave Act. Following a town meeting in support of Burns, there was a riot in which several people were injured and one person was killed. Burns was put on trial and on June 2 it was ruled that he had to be sent back to Colonel Suttle. Because of the anger of the citizens of Boston, Burns was escorted out of the city by twenty-two state militia to prevent any crowd violence. Over 50 000 people lined the streets to protest the decision and witness his transfer back to Suttle.

Burns was returned to Virginia where he was severely beaten and confined to a cage for months by Suttle. He was later sold to a plantation in North Carolina. Finally, members of the Black church he had attended in Boston purchased him and a matron financed his education at Oberlin College in Ohio as a student of religious studies. By 1860, Burns had moved to St. Catharines serving as the pastor of Zion Baptist Church on Geneva Street. He died on July 27, 1862, at the age of only 28, and is buried at Victoria Lawn Cemetery in St. Catharines. A plaque has been erected there honouring his courage and dedication and the fact that he was the last slave to be captured in Massachusetts.

On hearing that her father is to be tried for his part in assisting slaves to escape, Harriet declared,
"I just removed my father's trial to a higher court, and brought him off to Canada."

Disguises of the Underground Railroad

Passengers on the Underground Railroad often wore disguises to further throw off any suspicion. Sometimes women dressed as men, or a light-coloured slave might assume the role of a slave owner in order to travel with other darker freedom seekers. Elegant clothes belonging to free Blacks might be borrowed to give a fugitive the look of an affluent person. There were instances when a disguise might not have been enough to escape the reach of a search party, and individuals are known to have been hidden away until the intensity of the search seemed to be over. Sometimes it was months before they could continue on their journey to freedom.

According to Harriet's descendants, she often wore several layers of clothing, especially pantaloons, not only to protect herself from the cold and perhaps to appear heavier, but also to protect herself from the tracking dogs. If a dog were to chase Harriet as she was travelling with a party of escaping slaves, and if it were to bite her, it would be left with nothing but a mouthful of her clothing. She was concerned that these hounds not have the opportunity to taste her blood since she would then not be able to conduct successfully on the Underground Railroad – they would track her to death.

On her travels, Harriet might appear as a simple old woman with a flock of noisy chickens, as a slave travelling further south for her assumed master, or as just one of the many slaves in the area. Her demeanour and the way she carried herself were also important to her success – she would not have allowed herself to show fear or concern as her papers were being checked or as someone who could identify her came near. Her belief in the good of her cause gave her the resources to deal with all obstacles.

Letter from Thomas Garrett to J. Miller McKim:

Wilmington, December 29th, 1854

Esteemed Friend, J. Miller McKim: –
We made arrangements last night, and sent away Harriet Tubman, with six men and one woman to Allen Agnew's, to be forwarded across the country to the city. Harriet, and one of the men, had worn their shoes off their feet, and I gave them two dollars to help fit them out, and directed a carriage to be hired at my expense. I now have two more from the lowest county in Maryland, on the Peninsula, upwards of one hundred miles. I will try to get one of our trusty colored men to take them to-morrow morning to the Anti-Slavery office. You can pass them on.

Thomas Garrett

Routes of the Underground Railroad

Harriet did not always follow the same route to get to Canada, and sometimes she even travelled south in order to avoid suspicion if she felt she had been identified. She might arrange to meet her group during a new moon, when the darkness of the night would make the group more difficult to see. If enough money was available from "stockholders," she might purchase passage on the Philadelphia, Wilmington or Baltimore railroads or on a steamboat. But mostly, Harriet and her party travelled by foot and often wore out more than one pair of shoes that had been donated on their escape. She is known to have used stations in Camden, Dover, Blackbird, Middleton, New Castle, Wilmington, Laurel, Milford, Millsboro, Concord, Seaford, Smyrna, and Delaware City. She also used stations in Pennsylvania and New York State, including Syracuse, Auburn, Rochester and Niagara Falls.

Said of Joe, a nervous escapee Harriet was conducting:

"… From that time, Joe was silent; he talked no more; he sang no more; he sat with his head on his hand, and nobody could rouse him, nor make him take any interest in anything. After crossing the Suspension Bridge at Niagara Falls by train, Harriet said, "Joe! you've shook the lion's paw! Joe, you're in Queen Victoria's dominions! You're a free man!" While Harriet was caught up in the excitement of Joe's reaction to being free, he exclaimed, "Thank the Lord! there's only one journey for me now, and that's to Heaven!' "

Harriet had a premonition that slavery would be abolished. Three years later it was but she did not celebrate. When asked why, she explained, "I had my jubilee three years ago. I rejoiced all I could then; I can't rejoice no more."

Harriet is known to have crossed the railroad suspension bridge from Niagara Falls, New York, into Niagara Falls, Ontario, at least once. Given that it was such a well-patrolled crossing, however, and the fact that Harriet used many routes to transport her human cargo, it is unlikely that this was her only point of entry into Canada. The Niagara River, away from the Falls, is rather narrow, and many Underground Railroad stations existed all along the shores of Lake Ontario and Lake Erie. The Grand Island in the middle of the Niagara River provided a good point of entry: one could take a raft or boat from the western bank of the river to the western side of Grand Island, walk across the island, then float across the short distance on the eastern part of the river. There was also a well-organized ferry crossing between Buffalo, New York, and Fort Erie, Ontario, that could be used or that provided a route to follow. The Native people of the area crossed the river on rafts and may have guided or assisted freedom seekers. Harriet and other determined people would have to assess their situation.

The Suspension Bridge at Niagara Falls

The idea for a land connection between southern Ontario and Upper New York State was conceived by William Hamilton Merritt of St. Catharines. Merritt had been successful in building the Welland Canal and was interested in improving trade between the two countries. He felt that a land route would allow carriages access to the markets of St. Catharines, encourage more business on both sides of the border and attract tourist for the mineral spring spas. Merritt used his experience as financial agent for the Welland Canada Company to start the project.

A community, called Suspension Bridge, grew up near Drummondville at the north end of Niagara Falls, Ontario, and a similar settlement on the American side had the same name. Later the community referred to as Suspension Bridge became known as Niagara Falls, and today, Bridge Street marks the location of the centre of this community in Ontario. In 1849 the building of the suspension bridge was complete, with two levels combining a train bridge with a motor way, one over the other. Many escaping freedom-seekers crossed into Canada over the suspension bridge, which remains to this day.

The Moses of Her People

Because freedom seekers felt protected in Harriet's company and because she had been able to avoid capture, she came to be referred to as "Moses" freeing her people. As well, she earned the respect of Whites working in the abolition movement. Thomas Garrett said of her, "If she had been a White woman, she would have been heralded as the greatest woman of her age."

There was a pattern that Harriet followed. During the summer and winter, she would work to finance her travels into slaves states. Her rescues were done in the spring and fall of the year.

The number of people in her party varied from a small group of three to a group as large as 40. Discipline was very important to the success of the rescues, and the larger the group the greater the need for absolute control. Harriet was even known to threaten her charges with a gun to keep them under control.

Throughout her life, Harriet had a long connection with illness and healing. As a child, she had become seriously ill after

Niagara Suspention Bridge Crossing

Opened in 1849, the Niagara Suspension Bridge was the first of its kind in the world. This Bridge was built with two levels with the upper deck level for trains (bottom left) and a lower deck level for carriages and pedestrians (below right). It increased trade and tourism between the United States and Canada, and also provided another point of entry for freedom seekers. Perhaps there was no guard posted at the entrance to the lower level at night, or the guard looked the other way when Underground Railroad passengers needed to cross. This would have helped the use of the bridge and the choice of Niagara Falls and St. Catharines as terminals of the Underground Railroad. On at least one occasion, we know that Tubman with her human "cargo" took an actual train ride across the Suspension Bridge into Niagara Falls, Ontario, before heading to St. Catharines.

There were various places to cross the Niagara River. The Lewiston and Queenston bridge was opened in 1851 and the Niagara Railway Suspension Bridge followed in 1855. Other bridges, ferry routes or makeshift boats were utilized to enter the land for freedom. It could take as little as two weeks or as long as 9 weeks of constant night travel and hiding by day before a freedom seeker would reach a main crossing point into Canada.

tending the traps in the swamps. It was only her mother's knowledge of herbal medicine and her constant care that helped Harriet get better. Later, when Harriet was hit in the head with a 2-pound weight, it was her mother who again cared for her. When they were ill, slaves did not receive formal medical treatment and they had to rely on remedies and knowledge that had been brought from Africa. As well, some slaves had contact with Native people who taught them about the healing properties of certain North American plants.

Harriet taught her descendants about some of the healing plants and procedures that she had found effective. In one instance, a relative had an accident and her thumb was almost severed. Immediately, Harriet went to the barn and gathered some cobwebs and wrapped them around the injury, covering it with a handkerchief. This procedure was repeated every three days. After repeated treatment, the thumb healed without a scar.

Harriet is known to have prepared a poultice of poke salad (dandelion greens) which was placed on the foot to bring down swelling. For a cold, she would prepare a poultice of onions and camphorated oil which would be placed on the chest and covered with flannel. If the onion poultice was brown in the morning, that meant that the fever was broken.

For warts, Harriet would use the liquid from the milkweed plant and spread it on the warts. The procedure was repeated for three or four times until the wart finally disappeared.

Even today, some members of her family feel that she was aware of the properties of penicillin. If Harriet saw a mould form on the top of the foods that the family had canned in the harvest season, she would remove the mould, place it in another jar, add fresh lemon juice, honey and brandy and mix it together. Then if you got a cold, you would be given a teaspoon of this mixture that helped kill the bacteria.

In November 1856, Harriet returned to the Bucktown area to bring another group north. One member of this group was Josiah Bailey, who had cost his new owner $1000 down and $1000 to be paid later for his purchase. Although he had always been a loyal worker without a "behaviour" problem, Josiah was flogged on the very first day with his new master. Supposedly to teach him "respect," this beating convinced Josiah that he had had enough; he decided to run, joining Bill and Peter Pennington, Eliza Nokey and one other on board Harriet's train to freedom.

When it was discovered that they had fled, rewards were posted for their return. A reward of $1500 was offered for Josiah's

Raising funds was an important part of helping Blacks to freedom:

"I'm going to Mr. ____'s office, and I ain't going to leave there, and I ain't going to eat or drink, till I get money enough to take me down after the old people [her parents]."

She went into this gentleman's office.

"How do you do, Harriet? What do you want?" was the first greeting.

"I want some money, sir."

"You do! How much do you want?"

"I want twenty dollars, sir!"

"Twenty dollars! Who told you to come here for twenty dollars?"

"The Lord told me, sir."

"He did; well I guess the Lord's mistaken this time."

"No sir, the Lord's never mistaken! Anyhow I'm going to sit here until I get it."

(Harriet remained in the office, sometimes awake, sometimes asleep all day and possibly overnight…)

"…The sympathies of those visitors to the office were aroused; at all events she came to full consciousness, at last to find herself the happy possessor of sixty dollars, the contribution of these strangers. She went on her way rejoicing to bring her old parents from the land of bondage."

return, $800 for Peter, $300 for Bill and $1200 for Harriet herself. Additional rewards were advertised for Harriet's capture with each successful rescue mission. In spite of the posting of rewards and the search for the group, they safely arrived in the North. By June 1859, the Society of Slaveholders decided at their convention that there should be insurance policies to protect the slaveholders against the loss of their "property" through escapes. The society also offered a reward of $40 000 (equivalent to more than half a million dollars in current money) for the capture of Harriet Tubman. Harriet had become one of the most wanted people in the United States because of her success in conducting people to freedom.

In 1857, Harriet learned that her parents were suspected of having assisted with the escape of some slaves and were likely to be arrested for their part and put in jail. She had always wanted to rescue them, but she knew that they would probably not be sold further south because they would not earn much money on the auction block now that they were older. Now was the time to rescue them. With money from the New York Anti-Slavery office, Harriet went to Maryland and made a horse-drawn vehicle out of the remnants of an old buggy, boards, wheels and a harness made of straw. Her frail parents would thus be able to ride all night out of the Bucktown area and even take along some of the belongings they did not want to part with. Her mother prized her feather comforter and her father wanted to keep his broadaxe and other tools that would be useful in establishing a new home. In southern Delaware, Harriet was able to board a train to Wilmington where Thomas Garrett gave her enough money to buy their train passage to Canada and to safety in St. Catharines. Harriet now had freed all her family, except one sister and her children. Because of the heightened conflict between those who held slaves and those who were in favour of the abolition of slavery, Harriet was cautioned not to attempt any more rescues.

Codes and Secret Messages

Enslaved people were forbidden by law to congregate in groups except for religious services and nighttime funerals. Still, people managed to share information.

Those who worked in the master's house were able to learn of the master's family's travel or business plans. Those who worked in the fields were able to observe people who were travelling on the roads and who were trying to escape. Some slaves were able to share the stories of their experience in northern states or Canada while they travelled with their owners for the owner's business or vacation trip. But it was difficult to pass on any information and so the people developed signals in the form of meaningful stares and body language, as well as their own meanings for their songs and spirituals.

Some have said that Harriet Tubman would join a large group of field hands where she would not be noticed and as they toiled, she would let them know that she had connections to make them free. She would then arrange the meeting time and place, or signal them through song when it was time to go. Upon hearing Harriet sing "Swing Low, Sweet Chariot," freedom seekers would gather and join the singing so that it would be heard in neighbouring plantations to signal that the "freedom train" was ready to leave. When the owners finally realized that the spirituals carried special coded messages, they banned the people from singing them. By this time, however, other songs, whistles, or words with double meanings had replaced the spirituals.

New Beginnings

Upon making themselves free, former slaves sometimes gave themselves new names to conceal their identity and to reflect their new status as self-emancipated people. The surname "Freeman" was commonly used by many people. Some former slaves would rename themselves after political figures who had

Freedom seekers benefitted from the narrow Niagara River since they might be able to enter Canada on a makeshift raft if the bridge were being patrolled. It gave them hope on the last leg of their journey as they could see how close they were to freedom (top).

While there was no single means of crossing, just as there was no single starting point, freedom seekers in the Buffalo, New York, area might have made their way across the river to Fort Erie, Ontario. They would be encouraged by lantern signals or by abolitionists who would meet them as they arrived safely on the other side. They could continue to travel or possibly be escorted into Bertie Hall, a "safe house" (below left). This large home was owned by the Forsyth family, who were well known as smugglers and it is believed that the family had a tunnel built between the river and the house to carry the smuggled goods. It is also considered that Bertie Hall was used as a safe house for fugitive slaves who were kept in the basement (bottom right) until they could be taken farther from the border to safety.

In this area, they might be escorted to nearby "Little Africa" and often the people got their new start working in the shipyard located there. The forests of black walnut, oak and ash provided employment for Blacks in Little Africa until the wood reserves were exhausted. With diminished work opportunities the people moved to new areas and by the beginning of the twentieth century Little Africa no longer existed.

supported anti-slavery measures, or they would assume common names unlike the often-biblical names they had been given when they were enslaved. Someone known as "Ezekiel" in Virginia might become Charles Johnson in Philadelphia and possibly John Freeman in Canada.

Blacks entering Canada as fugitives from the repressive laws or as freedom seekers were cautioned not to tell anyone what their true identity was and not to speak about where they were originally from or of the family they had left behind. This was to protect them from bounty hunters and their agents who might even cross the border into Canada in the search. Escape stories might be passed down within families, but the fear of recapture was very real. Some survivors kept their freedom papers if they had been granted their freedom, just in case they might have a problem or a chance to return. Sadly, most individuals took their escape stories with them to the grave.

According to oral history, Harriet kidnapped the daughter of one of her brothers, eight-year-old Margaret, and boarded her with William Seward, a politician in Auburn, New York. Harriet may have felt that she would be able to ensure security for Margaret and provide her a more normal childhood, unlike the experiences that she herself had had at the same age.

The Last Trip

Harriet's last known trip on the Underground Railroad may have been the one she made in December 1860 when she tried to find her sister in Maryland. The sister had, in fact, died, so Harriet took seven others with her. In all Harriet made 19 trips on the Underground Railroad, without losing any of her 300 or more passengers and none of them were recaptured.

Later, towards the end of 1858, Harriet moved her parents from St. Catharines to Auburn, New York. She made her home there about the same time because Auburn was becoming a centre for abolitionists and the women's suffrage movement – which was of interest to Harriet. Also, their granddaughter, Margaret, was living there.

Harriet may have come to realize that as important as her assistance might be to a small group of fleeing slaves, it was time to widen the assistance on a larger scale. In her 19 life-risking missions, Harriet had rescued over 300 people, but there were thousands of others still suffering. Even if she spent the rest of her life conducting people to safety, she would never be able to free them all. A larger movement or political reform that would end slavery began to have great appeal to her.

Frederick Douglass had introduced William Seward to her. Seward was a Republican who had opposed the Fugitive Slave Act and had been close to winning a presidential election. He had supported the John Brown slave rebellion at Harpers Ferry, however, and that had cost him a victory in the election. Nonetheless, Seward continued his support for freedom and he assisted Harriet in her bid to purchase land in Auburn. In fact, some reports indicate that he had loaned Harriet the money to buy property in Auburn, which she later repaid with

Harriet Tubman: "I have seen hundreds of escaped slaves, but I never saw one who was willing to go back and be a slave."

the proceeds from the sale of the Sarah Bradford book, *Scenes in the Life of Harriet Tubman.*

With the failure at Harpers Ferry, John Brown was sentenced to death for treason and was hanged. Osborne Anderson, who was the only Black from Canada to join Brown on the raid and the only one to survive, later wrote of the experience in the book *A Voice From Harpers Ferry* that the raid did not go according to plan. A White recruit from Chatham defected and told of the plans which caused a delay in the raid. Communication problems prevented a number of attackers from getting to the area in time – only 20 took part in the raid. While there had been at least 250 slave revolts in the United States by the time of Brown's raid, this was one of the first that was led by Whites. By his action, Brown raised fear among Whites and forced people to take a stand on slavery, thereby widening the gap between the industrial, anti-slavery North and the agricultural, pro-slavery South. It marked a significant turning point in relations between the Union and Confederacy which precipitated the American Civil War.

One of Harriet's planned meetings with John Brown in 1858 did not happen. She did not appear at Daly House, at the corner of Oxford and King streets in Ingersoll. Brown wrote to W. H. Day, a contact in St. Catharines, to find out why the meeting had not taken place and learned that coincidentally Harriet had been on the same train that Brown had been on. She was in fact, watching him to confirm his dedication.

Throughout the spring of 1859, Harriet had spent time recruiting men to serve with John Brown's forces, but she was too ill to assist him at the time of his raid. She was recuperating in New Bedford when the raid on Harpers Ferry

Frederick Douglass

As a self-emancipated Black man, Douglass worked for the Anti-Slavery Society in New Bedford, Massachusetts. He gave many speaking engagements on slavery and travelled in Great Britain on an extended lecture tour for a couple of years to purchase his freedom. He then began to publish his newspaper, the *North Star*, for Blacks. He strongly wanted Blacks to stay in the United States, but this did not prevent him from assisting those who wanted to make themselves free. He was very active in the Underground Railroad and personally helped to conceal, feed and shelter escaping slaves.

took place. As soon as she was able after the raid, Harriet and Frederick Douglass and a few others left for Canada because the community was so agitated by the raid on Harpers Ferry. Despite her absence from the raid itself, Harriet was identified as a co-conspirator through the media and investigations that followed.

John Brown

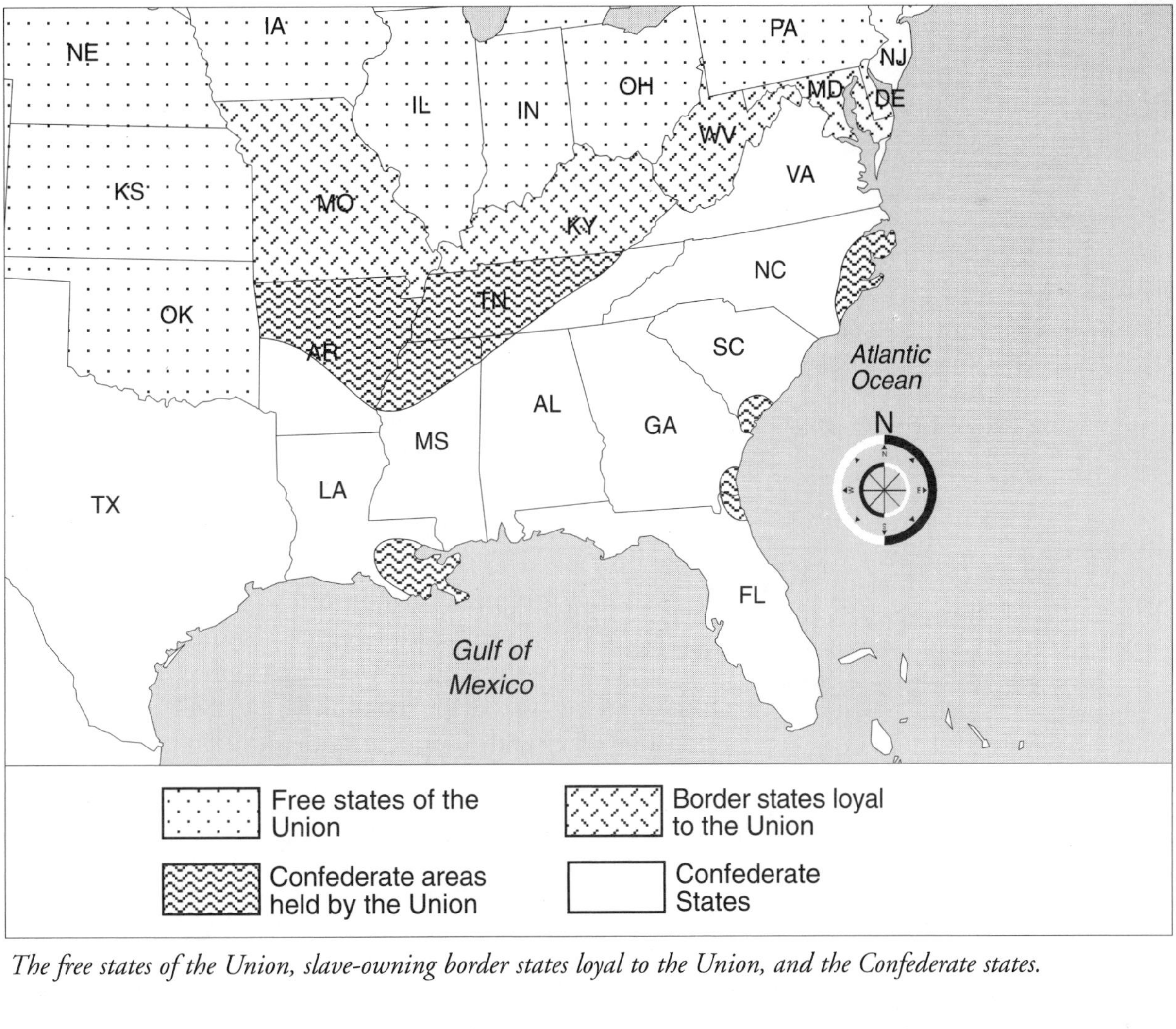

Free states of the Union

Border states loyal to the Union

Confederate areas held by the Union

Confederate States

The free states of the Union, slave-owning border states loyal to the Union, and the Confederate states.

Chapter Six

Return to the United States

With the beginning of the Civil War, Harriet was not able to continue with her rescue of slaves. However, she continued to feel compelled to assist the cause in any way she could. In April 1861, in an interview with John Andrews, Governor of Massachusetts and a supporter of John Brown, Harriet was invited to join the Union forces at Hilton Head, South Carolina. Because she preferred to be outdoors, she welcomed this chance to help. Her first assignment was to nurse the wounded with the First and Second Carolina Regiments. Later she served as a spy for the North, and by 1863, she had organized what today would be called an Intelligence Service, choosing former slaves who knew the countryside and could guide the forces. The information gathered by Harriet provided significant assistance to the Union forces.

One of the most famous raids of the Civil War was the raid on the Combahee River, South Carolina, in 1863 to destroy those plantations that had been supplying food to the Confederate side. The Black scouts knew where the mine traps were set in the river, and through the information provided by Harriet and her spies, the Union forces of over 300 were able to avoid the mines. Former enslaved field hands piloted gunboats down the river and burned crops and buildings as directed by Harriet. Over 750 slaves were freed in the raid and Harriet was credited as the leader who planned the strategy and made it such a success. In doing so, Harriet was the first and only woman in American history to lead a military assault. F. B. Sanborn, Secretary of the Massachusetts Board of State charities and a supporter of John Brown, said of her, "She has accomplished her purposes with a coolness, foresight, patience and wisdom, which in a White man would have raised him to the highest pitch of reputation."

Harriet assisted in any manner that was required. She continued her service to the Union forces by cooking, doing laundry and carrying dispatches for various units in the field. She served at the battle in Charleston Harbour, spring 1864, and described this battle which ended with the death of 1500 Black troops:

> Then we saw the lightening and that was the guns; and then we heard the thunder, and that was the big guns; and then we heard the rain falling, and that was the drops of blood falling; and when we came to get in the crops, it was dead men that we reaped.

In the spring of 1864 she requested a leave of absence from the war and returned to Auburn to rest. It was during this period in Auburn that Sarah Bradford interviewed her for her book, *Scenes in the Life of Harriet Tubman,* that is the closest to an authoritative biography of Harriet prepared during her lifetime.

After her brief rest in Auburn, she was again well enough to travel to Boston to meet Sojourner Truth, the 67-year old, outspoken supporter of Women's rights, abolition and religious freedom. She also met with William Seward, who by this time was Secretary of State. She declined to meet President Abraham Lincoln, partly because she didn't feel he had done enough to free slaves and partly because she agreed with other Black leaders who criticized Lincoln for not declaring the goal of the Civil War was to end slavery. Also, the President had not accepted Blacks in the Union Army – until 1863. In fact, Harriet felt that John Brown had done more for the cause of establishing freedom than Lincoln.

Harriet Tubman only had her strong will and a pistol or sharpened clam shells on her Underground Railroad missions. During the Civil War, Tubman, the scout and spy, often had a rifle.

"I am confident that she is not only truthful, but that she has a rare discernment, and a deep and sublime philanthropy."

June 13, 1868, *Frederick Douglass*

Early in 1865, near the end of the war, Harriet agreed to assist Martin Delaney to recruit and train a Black military unit drawn from the South. Although plans were in place for such a unit, the war ended on April 9 when General Robert E. Lee, General-in-Chief of the Confederate Armies, signed the surrender agreement with Ulysses S. Grant, leader of the Union forces, at Appomatox. However, there were still ways Harriet was needed, such as aiding the wounded. After the war, she served at Fort Munroe, Virginia, and later at Fernadina, Florida, where she was appointed "Matron," or superintendent, of the hospital. For all her contributions throughout the war, she received only $200, which was given to her in 1862.

Sojourner Truth

Born in 1797 and named Isabella Van Wagoner, a slave in Hurley , New York, she lived to see most of her 13 children sold into slavery. She was a tall, impressive woman who became involved with abolitionists and was a staunch supporter of President Lincoln, whom she credits with freeing the slaves. She was deeply religious and took the name Sojourner Truth to reflect her numerous presentations on the need for temperance, the abolition of slavery, and women's rights. She strongly supported the movement of Blacks to the West, particularly to Kansas and Missouri.

Harriet's Later Life

After the war, Harriet wanted to see her family, so with her government pass entitling her to pay half-fare on the train, she left the hospital and headed for Auburn, where her family lived. On the trip north, some of the passengers were offended by her presence, even though she had paid for her seat. They questioned how a Black person could have a government pass. The ticket taker and several others insulted her, grabbed her and threw her into the baggage compartment, badly hurting her arm. What injustice! Harriet had survived the war only to receive a war injury on her way home after the war had ended. Ironically, about the same time, William Garrison, a White anti-slavery abolitionist, was receiving $30,000 for his anti-slavery work.

Thirteenth Amendment

Slavery was finally abolished in the United States with the adoption of the Thirteenth Amendment of the Constitution of the United States on December 18, 1865.

Section 1. Neither slavery nor involuntary servitude, except as a punishment for crime whereof the party shall have been duly convicted, shall exist within the United States, or any place subject to their jurisdiction.

Section 2. Congress shall have power to enforce this article by appropriate legislation.

Clearly, despite the Thirteenth Amendment to the Constitution, which freed the slaves in the Union territory, the treatment and experience of Blacks was still far from fair and equitable. Her estranged husband, John Tubman, had an argument in 1867 with Rob Vincent, a White man, in Dorchester County over some ashes. Vincent threatened to kill John and when the two met accidentally later that same day, Vincent stopped his wagon, turned and deliberately fired at him, killing John immediately. Two witnesses saw what had happened, one being John Tubman's 13-year old son. Vincent was arrested, tried in court but unbelievably found not guilty.

While living in Auburn, Harriet supported herself by working as a nurse, cooking for others, taking care of children, raising chickens, growing vegetables for sale and generally doing anything possible to maintain her independence. She did this not just for herself, but she had to support 20 people, including her parents, her brother William Henry, her nephew (Harkless Bowley) and a grand-niece (Eva Stewart). As well, if she had received what she was entitled to for her work with the government during the war, estimated to be $18 000 – plus an additional amount for her recruiting activity – she would have been able to live comfortably. She did receive some money from the sale of the book by Sarah Bradford on her life, but it was a relatively small amount.

A rare formal photograph of Harriet Tubman taken in Auburn. Tubman became active with suffragettes and made many speeches about women's rights.

One day, a man appeared at her door. His name was Nelson Davis and he claimed to have met her during the war, in 1864, while he was a member of the 8th Colored Infantry. He admired Harriet and what she had accomplished. He was 20 years younger than Harriet and although he looked healthy, he was unable to work because of the tuberculosis he had contracted. All her life, Harriet had a personal commitment to help others and may have been flattered by his admiration – or she might have felt a need to protect him because he was ill. Maybe the two just fell in love. They courted and were wed in Central Church, Auburn, on March 18, 1869. They lived together until Nelson finally died from tuberculosis nearly twenty years later in 1888.

Harriet Tubman with some of those she guided to freedom. As well, the man seated on her left is reputed to be Nelson Davis, her husband.

In August 1868, Harriet received a letter from her old friend, Frederick Douglass. In the letter Douglass acknowledges her lifelong sacrifices and dedication to helping others:

> The difference between us is very marked. The most that I have done and suffered in the service of our cause has been in public, and I have received much encouragement every step of the way. You, on the other hand, have laboured in a private way. I have wrought in the day – you in the night. I have had the applause of the crowd and the satisfaction of being approved by the multitude, while the most that you have done has been witnessed by a few trembling, scared and foot-sore bondsmen and women, whom you have led out of the house of bondage, and whose heartfelt, 'God bless you' has been your only reward. The midnight sky and the silent stars have been the witness of your devotion to freedom.

Obviously, she was touched by this recognition from a friend who had shared her dedication in freeing enslaved people.

"I know of no one who has willingly encountered more perils and hardships to serve our enslaved people than you have...I regard you in every way truthful and trustworthy."

Aug. 29, 1868. *Gerrit Smith*

The Harriet Tubman Home in Auburn, New York, is now operated by the AME Zion Church as a historic site.

This recognition came from others as well who valued her contribution. Over the years, certain citizens of Auburn had made donations to her and she had accumulated some proceeds from the sale of the book on her life by Sarah Bradford. Finally, in 1896, she was able to purchase an adjacent property (26 acres, 10 ha.) next to her home in Auburn. There were two buildings already erected on the property and it was valued at $6000 with a mortgage of $1700. Initially, she had planned to pay off the mortgage and open a home for young girls. However, later on, she decided that it would be better to leave the property as a home for the aged, and in 1908 the John Brown Home was opened and deeded the property to the AME Zion Church of Auburn for this purpose. Finally, in 1903, The Harriet Tubman Home for Aged and Indigent Colored People was incorporated and the home was formally opened in 1908. In fact, Harriet lived there for the last two years of her life. Today, the AME Zion Church keeps Harriet's dream alive for a home for the aged and a meeting place for the young through public support.

In 1888, the United States Congress passed an act giving the widows of Civil War veterans a pension of $8 a month. Harriet, now the widow of Nelson Davis, resubmitted her petition for payment for her three years of service as a nurse, cook and scout commander, but she was not successful. Finally she was granted the widow's pension of $8 a month and in 1899 this was increased to $20 a month. But she was denied a full military pension of her own.

Her reputation was once taken advantage of by men who sought to profit at her expense. Her brother told her about a money-making scheme he had heard about and hoped that, with the influential contacts that Harriet had, they could undertake a profitable venture. Apparently, two Black men claimed they had

Harriet Tubman

Born a slave in Maryland about 1821.
Died in Auburn, N.Y., March 10th, 1913
Called the Moses of her people,
During the Civil War,
With rare courage She led over three hundred
Negroes up from slavery to freedom,
and rendered invaluable service
as nurse and spy.
with implicit trust in God
She braved every danger
and overcame every obstacle,
Withal
She possessed extraordinary
foresight and judgment so that
She truthfully said,
"On my Underground Railroad
I nebber run my train off de track
An' I nebber los' a passenger."

This tablet is erected
By the Citizens of Auburn.

found gold that had been hidden during the Civil War in the South so that it would not be confiscated by the enemy. Now that the war was over their plan was to sell the gold they had found for money and promised Harriet that she would be able to have a sizable portion of the profits for her assistance. Harriet's credibility was high and she was quickly able to convince the affluent business leaders of Auburn of the worth of the plan, receiving $2000 for her participation. It was too awkward to convert the gold in the South where it had been found, so at the appointed time she set out for a nearby spot with two others to exchange the gold for currency. On her way, Harriet was attacked and was forcibly bound and gagged; and neither the gold nor the money remained. She had planned to use the money to buy a home for Blacks in need, but her dream for the home was lost.

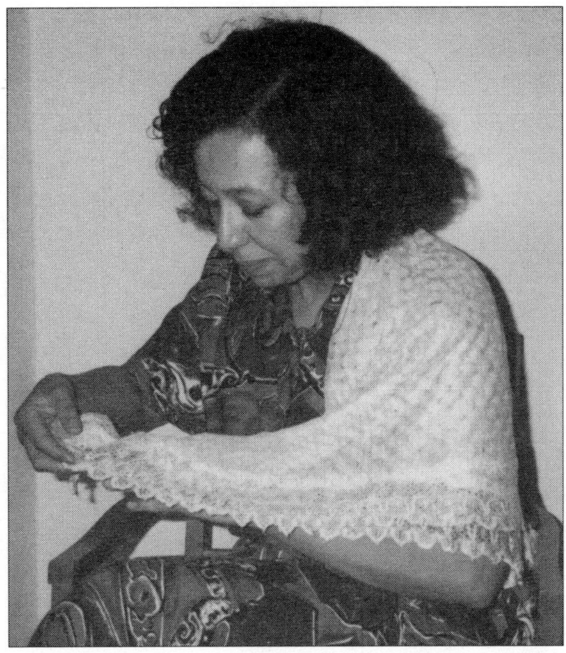

The author, Rosemary Sadlier, is shown examining the scarf presented to Harriet Tubman by Queen Victoria. Tubman took great pride in this gift and wore the scarf during her final years.

Undaunted, Harriet became active in the community. At the age of over 78 years, she was supporting the growth of the African Methodist Episcopal Church (AME), although she attended the White Central Church. She attended the National Association of Colored Women's Conference and in 1897 was invited to the Diamond Jubilee celebration of Queen Victoria's 60th year of reign in England. When she was in England, Harriet received a medal and a silk shawl from Queen Victoria which she treasured greatly. On her return, a benefit party was held for her by the suffragettes of Boston. With the money raised there, as well as the proceeds from the sale of the second edition of her book, and money from the citizens of Auburn, Harriet finally was able to purchase the land for her home for Blacks next to her own house. In 1908, this became the Harriet Tubman Home for Aged and Indigent Negroes. In time the home was deeded to the AME Zion Church and today operates as a historical site and library in the name of Harriet Tubman.

Although she was once strong and active, in her later years Harriet was confined to a wheelchair because of the severity of her rheumatism and the frequency of her sleeping spells. She contracted pneumonia and died on March 10, 1913. She was buried at Fort Hill Cemetery in Auburn with the medal from Queen Victoria, and the place of her burial was marked with a marble headstone donated by the National Association of Colored Women. Veterans of the Civil War fired a volley over her grave as a tribute to her for her military service. On July 12, 1914, as an act of respect, the citizens of Auburn unveiled a plaque to Harriet on the courthouse of the District of Cayuga in a ceremony that included a special tribute delivered by

Booker T. Washington. And in Bucktown, Maryland, a historical sign marks the spot where Harriet received her head injury long ago – the site of the Bucktown store. Further signs of respect for her contributions included the christening of the ship the *S.S. Harriet Tubman* in the 1940s. In 1978, the United States Postal Service issued its first stamp in the Black Heritage USA Series commemorating the life of Harriet Tubman.

Harriet Tubman (centre) surrounded by friends and supporters on the grounds of the Harriet Tubman Home.

In July 1993, the province of Ontario erected a historical plaque dedicated to Harriet Tubman on the grounds of the St. Catharines branch of the British Methodist Episcopal Church of Canada. In ceremonies leading up to the unveiling, government officials, descendants of freedom seekers and relatives of Harriet Tubman joined together to celebrate her achievements and her legacy of inspiration.

A Rich Legacy

As the most successful conductor on the Underground Railroad, Harriet was able to bring over 300 people safely to Canada in her many rescue trips. Exact records, of course, were not kept but it is likely that she brought even more than that number. Later in life, Harriet hinted that she, in fact, made more than 19 rescue trips. This alone was a significant accomplishment considering the severe penalties for even reading about abolition in the United States in those days. Every time Harriet helped an enslaved person become a free person she was committing a crime: by her action, she was costing the plantation owners money with their loss of the labour of their slaves. She was disrupting the system and was using Canada as a safe haven. Every rescue was an anti-slavery statement. And as if Harriet's own personally escorted rescue missions were not successful enough, her reputation inspired others to take the risk of free-

This was the first stamp in the Black Heritage USA series. Issued in 1978, it honoured Harriet Tubman for her struggle as an abolitionist, nurse and escaped slave.

ing themselves or of going back to their former plantations to lead their families to freedom.

The Underground Railroad was critical for the freedom seekers. It heightened the debate between slave-holding interests and those who promoted abolition. Had Canada not been willing to grant the same rights and privileges to Blacks as to members of other groups, and had it not been in such close proximity to the Americans, there probably would have been fewer Underground Railroad survivors in Canada. In the pioneer society of English-speaking southern Ontario especially, conditions supported the entry and security of freedom seekers. The climate, economy and language were similar to that of the northern United States without the constant threat of being recaptured.

Mariline Wilkins proudly displays items used by Harriet Tubman and passed down through the family.

Many Blacks were able to express the positive experiences of their freedom in Canada through their writing or speaking engagements. Among them were Mary Ann Shadd, Frederick Douglass, Reverend Samuel Ringgold Ward, Henry Bibb, and Josiah Henson. They were concerned about highlighting their successes because pro-slavery interests promoted the notion that people of African descent could not take care of themselves, would be unable to lead wholesome lives, were incapable of learning and actually needed slavery to protect them from themselves. These Black abolitionists portrayed the free Black community in a positive way, showing that Blacks were not only competent and capable but also interested in taking care of themselves. Abolitionists travelled throughout the North and South speaking wherever they could find an audience, sharing information about how well the Blacks in Canada were managing, and how they too could join or support other Blacks in getting to Canada. They told of the success of the Black population of Ontario, in particular, who were praised as a beacon of hope that free Blacks could thrive and make a contribution. If they could live free, productive lives in Canada, surely others could do the same in the United States once slavery was ended.

On June 6, 1944, a ship, the S.S. Harriet Tubman, *was launched at South Portland, Maine. The first ship to be named for an African American, Tubman's descendant, Mariline Wilkins holds the boxed bottle which was used to christen the ship at the launch.*

The successful presence of Blacks in Canada, the holding of the North American Free Men's Convention in Toronto and Harriet Tubman's work and residence in Canada, combined with the protection of the rights of Blacks under law in Canada, created an affront to those who supported slavery. Although the laws did not support slavery, the laws could not force people to view Blacks as equals and therefore treat them equitably. The survival of Black people in Canada was not always easy despite the glowing reports of abolitionists. Black Canadians had to fight for their rights and where their numbers were small, they had to find other ways to achieve their goals by creating their own churches, schools, and organizations, or by co-operating and compromising with others.

With the beginning of the Civil War, Harriet was not able to continue her rescue of slaves and bring them to freedom. Instead, she recognized that there were other avenues that she could use to help the cause. She joined the Union forces, recruited men to serve in the conflict and later dedicated herself to nursing those who had suffered in battle.

Harriet Tubman's dedication, commitment and courage, her ability to persevere no matter what the obstacles and her genuine concern for others show her to be a woman who made a difference – to Blacks, to abolitionists and to North American history. Her example compelled others to forge their own freedom train or to assert themselves in dynamic ways and she was an inspiration to others: if this woman could succeed, many felt that they too could succeed.

With the financial support of Tubman descendants and supporters, this Freedom Park *at the corner of North and Dill Streets, Auburn, was created to ensure that the legacy of her work is widely known.*

Last Will and Testament

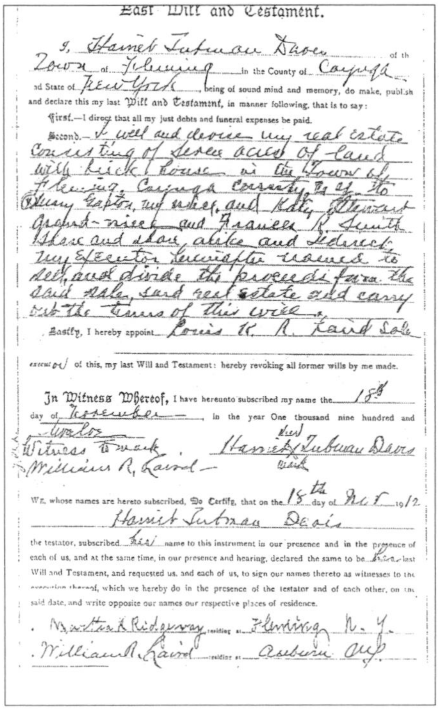

I, Harriet Tubman Davis of the Town of Fleming in the County of Cayuga and State of New York, being of sound mind and memory, do make, publish and declare this my last Will and Testament, in manner following, that is to say:

First. – I direct that all my just debts and funeral expenses be paid.

Second. – I will and devise my real estate consisting of seven acres of land with brick house in the Town of Fleming, Cayuga County, to Mary Gaskin, my niece, and Kathy Stewart, grand-niece and Frances R. Smith [to] share and share alike and direct my Executor hereinafter named to sell and divide the proceeds from the said sale, said real estate and carry out the terms of this will.

Lastly, I hereby appoint Louis K. R. Laird sole executor of this, my last Will and Testament: hereby revoking all former wills by me made.

In Witness Whereof, I have hereunto subscribed my name the 18th day of November in the year One thousand nine hundred and twelve.

her

Witness to mark, Harriet X Tubman
William R. Laird

mark

We, whose names are hereto subscribed, do certify, that on the 18th day of Nov. 1912 Harriet Tubman Davis the testator, subscribed her name to this instrument in our presence and in the presence of each of us, and at the same time, in our presence and hearing, declared the same to be her last Will and Testament, and requested us, and each of us, to sign our names thereto as witnesses to the execution thereof, which we hereby do in the presence of the testator and of each other, on the said date and write opposite our names our respective places of residence.

Martha R. Ridgeway residing at Fleming N. Y.

William R. Laird residing at Auburn, N. Y.

Affidavit

Sworn by Harriet Tubman
November 10, 1894

State of New York
County of Cayuga

In the matter of original Pension no. 449,592 of Harriet Davis as Widow of Nelson Davis late of Co. "G" 8th Reg't U.S.C.T. on this 10th day of Nov. 1894 personally appeared before me. Harriet Davis who is well known to me to be entitled to full credit and belief and who being by unduly sworn deposes and says in relation to the aforesaid case as follows:

I was born in Cambridge, Dorchester County, Md.

My residence at the time I became acquainted with the above named soldier, was in the Town of Fleming, Cayuga Co.[County], N.Y. (adjoining the city of Auburn, N.Y.). My P.O. address was then and is now Auburn, Cayuga Co.[County], N.Y. There has been no change of my P.O. address nor residence since.

I had known the soldier before my marriage to him a little over three years.

I was married to the soldier in the city of Auburn, N.Y., March 18th 1869 by the Rev. Henry Fowler. See proof of my marriage on file.

I was a slave in the state of Maryland before the war. My owner's name was Edward Broadice [sometimes spelled Brodas or Brodess, editor]. I escaped from slavery before the war and came North. I was not a slave at the time of my marriage to the soldier, I having been freed by the Proclamation of President Lincoln.

My name before I married my first husband John Tubman was Harriet Ross. After my marriage to him my name was Harriet Tubman and so continued and I was known and recognized by that name until my marriage to Nelson Davis. See affidavit of Nov. 28, 1892 and proof of J. Tubman's death dated Nov. 22nd, 1892 all on file with my claim. I have had no husband since the death of the soldier, Nelson Davis.

I have no knowledge as to how he enlisted (or was drafted) but I have heard him say it was at Oneida or Rome, Oneida Co. [County] N.Y. I have his certificate of discharge which shows that he was enrolled Sept. 25, 1863 and discharged at Brownsville, Texas, Nov. 10, 1865 and did not re-enlist.

I never had any children nor child by the soldier nor by John Tubman.

The soldier was born (as he informed me) in or near Elizabeth City, North Carolina. His actual residence when I became acquainted with him was at my house in the town of Fleming, Cayuga Co. [County] N.Y. as a boarder and so continued to live until the date of our marriage and continued to live at the same place as my husband till he died, Oct. 14, 1888, during all of that his P.O. address was Auburn, Cayuga Co [County], N.Y. and we were never divorced from each other. I have no knowledge of his change of residence before his enrollment as I did not [know] him till after he was discharged from the service and came to my house to live.

His occupation was that of a brickmaker and laborer. His age as given in the certificate of discharge is 21 and in the record of death it is 44. See proof of death on file. His height 5 ft. 11 inches, color of skin black.

The name of his owner (when a slave) was Fred Charles. His father's name was Milford Davis.

The soldier was not a slave at the time of his marriage to me nor at the time of his enrollment he having been freed from slavery by the Proclamation of President Lincoln Sept. 22, 1862 which gave him his freedom on January 1st, 1863. He was known as Nelson Charles and Nelson Davis. He never had any other wife but me. See proof upon this point on file with the claim, and my affidavit of Nov. 28, 1892.

See my affidavit of Febr'y [February] 1st 1892 showing the character, location, extent and value of my property real and personal owned or possessed by me, also the affidavit of William H. Stewart _____ Washington of July 21, 1892.

There has been but little change in the character and extent of my property since my former _____. Except my horse has since died and the mortgage of two hundred has been increased to five hundred. See certificate of C.G. Adams of Sept. 4, 1894.

There is no one legally bound for my support.

her
Harriet X Tubman
mark

(witness)Helen M. Windover
S. J. Westfall

Subscribed and sworn to before me this 10 day of Nov. 1894 and I certify that I have no interest or bias in any matter to which this relates.

C. G. Adams
Clerk of County Court of
Cayuga County New York

An Acrostic Describing my Great Great Aunt
A Tribute to Harriet Tubman

Humble, heroic, honorable
Admirable, afflicted
Rugged, reputable
Real, reliable, religious (with a personal relationship with God)
Indomitable, ingenious, instinctive
Energetic, entrepreneur
Tough, but tender

Trustworthy, tireless
Underground Railroad conductor, undaunted
Bible believing, brave
Militant, but merciful
Acclaimed, activist; called Araminta as a child
Naturalist, nurse (in the Union Army)

Betty (Barnes) Browne
Great Grand Niece

The Harriet Tubman Home

Just before the beginning of the Civil War, Harriet purchased a seven-acre lot of land on South Street at the city of Auburnís city limits. To support herself and the others who lived with her there, she had to work hard to pay the expenses.

The money she received from the sale of the Sarah Bradford book on her life assisted in paying some of the mortgage on the property and by the time of the second printing of her biography in 1886, she purchased a second lot of 25 acres adjoining her original property. Since she had not yet been awarded a pension of her own or a widow's pension, she tried to pay for the property from the receipts of the sale of the book and donations from the people of Auburn. Certainly, as a senior citizen it would have been difficult for Harriet to earn sufficient money through her labours or even to seek donations for the maintenance of her property. Neither of these measures provided enough money but she did manage to obtain a bank loan on the land.

Harriet now owned two adjoining parcels of land and in her Will she directed her lawyer and heirs to sell her land and to divide the proceeds among her heirs equally. Following her death, the seven-acre property was sold to England Norris who divided the property and a small section was sold to Frank Norris. To this day, numbers 208 and 210 South Street remain in the Norris family.

Harriet sold the larger property to the AME Zion Church in 1903. Today, located at 180-182 South Street, the AME Zion Church owns and operates the Harriet Tubman Home on this 25-acre lot.

The Harriet Tubman Home in Auburn, New York, is operated by the AME Zion Church.

Surrogate's Court of the County of Cayuga

The Petition of Louis K. R. Laird of the City of Auburn County of Cayuga and State of New York, respectfully shows:

That Harriet Tubman Davis late of the Town of Fleming in the County of Cayuga aforesaid, departed this life on the 10th day of March in the year of our Lord, one thousand nine hundred thirteen

The said deceased was at the time of her death, a resident of the Town of Fleming in the County of Cayuga;

Said deceased left a Last Will and Testament, which is dated the 18th day of November in the year of our Lord one thousand nine hundred and twelve [xxxxxxxxxxxxxxxx xxxxxxx xxxxx [ ] Your petitioner is the executor named in said Will. The said deceased left no husband his widow, [xxxxxxxxxx xxxxxx xxxxxxxxxxxxxxxx The following named persons are the only heirs-at-law and next-of-kin of said deceased, and their degree of relationship to the said deceased, their places of residence and postoffice addresses are respectively as follows, viz.:

Charles Stewart,	a	Grand nephew	, who resides at	Auburn	State of	N. Y.
Alida Stewart,	a	Grand niece	, who resides at	Auburn	State of	N. Y.
Katy Stewart,	a	Grand niece	, who resides at	Auburn	State of	N. Y.
Clarence Stewart,	a	Grand nephew	, who resides at	Auburn	State of	N. Y.
Mary Gaston,	a	niece	, who resides at	Auburn	State of	N. Y.
Margaret Lucas,	a	grand niece	, who resides at	Auburn	State of	N. Y.
Gertrude Robinson,	a	Grand niece	, who resides at	Buffalo	State of	N. Y.
Elija Stewart,	a	nephew	, who resides at	Boston	State of	Mass.
Harkless Bowles,	a	nephew	, who resides at	Washington	State of	D. C.
Mary Stewart,	a	niece	, who resides at	St. Catherines	State of	Canada
Gertrude Thompson,	a	niece	, who resides at	St. Catherines	State of	Canada
Amanda Gales,	a	niece	, who resides at	St. Catherines	State of	Canada
Carrie Barnes	a	niece	, who resides at	Cayuga	State of	Canada
Mary Youngs	a	niece	, who resides at	St. Catherines	State of	Canada
	a		, who resides at		State of	
	a		, who resides at		State of	

That all the above named persons are of full age and sound mind, xxxxxxxxxxxxxxxxxxxxxxxxxxxxxxxxxx xxxxxxxxxxxxxxxxxxxxxxx

This is the official death certificate of Harriet Tubman and includes the names of several of her relatives who were living at the time of her death.

Chronology of Significant Related Events

1775 British forces led by Lord Dunmore invite enslaved Black men to join the British side against the Americans in the War of Independence.

1776 The Quakers declare that they will not own slaves.

1779 Sir Henry Clinton, leader of the British forces, invites all Black men, women, and children to join the British side and promises them freedom.

1787 Anti-slavery legislation is passed in the American Northwest Territories, which then include Illinois, Indiana, Iowa, Wisconsin and Michigan. By this time, Connecticut, Massachusetts, Pennsylvania, Rhode Island and Vermont have already passed anti-slavery laws.

1790 The parliament of Great Britain enacts *The Act for Encouraging New Settlers in His Majesties Colonies and Plantations in America,* encouraging Whites to settle in Canada with their enslaved Africans and household effects.

1793 The *Upper Canada Abolition Act* supported by Lieutenant-Governor Simcoe frees any slave who came into the province (now Ontario) and makes any person born of a slave mother free upon reaching age 25.

The first Fugitive Slave Act is passed in the United States. With the passage of this Fugitive Slave Act, by freedom seekers accelerates and the "Underground Railroad" begins.

1803 The Chief Justice of Lower Canada, William Osgoode, declares that slavery is inconsistent with British law.

1812 The Cochrane Proclamation invites refugees of the War of 1812 to become British citizens through residence in British possessions, including Canada, parts of the West Indies and Bermuda.

The Black settlement of Oro, Ontario, is established by the government for Black veterans who fought on the British side in the War of 1812. This is the only government-sponsored settlement in Ontario.

1820 Harriet Tubman is born about this date – the exact date of her birth is not known.

1822 Denmark Vesey, a slave in Charleston, South Carolina, plans a slave uprising but is prevented from carrying it out.

1827 Levi Coffin, a Quaker and a leading stationmaster on the Underground Railroad, begins his assistance to freedom seekers in Cincinnati, Ohio. He is often referred to as the "President" of the Underground Railroad.

1828 In Vermont, William Lloyd Garrison publishes *The Liberator*, an abolitionist newspaper.

1831 Nat Turner, a slave in Southampton County, Virginia, leads a slave rebellion in which 55 Whites are killed. Turner and the others who joined the rebellion are caught, tried and seventeen are hung and seven deported; but many other slaves are killed by the militia in putting down the rebels. As a result, Southerners become fearful of further uprisings by Blacks.

1833 The British Imperial Act abolishes slavery throughout the British Empire effective Aug. 1, 1834. This Act includes Canada, leading to the perception that Canada might be a safe haven for escaping slaves.

1837 Solomon Moseby, an escaped slave who reached Ontario, is seized by a bounty hunter but is prevented from being sent back to the United States when hundreds of free Black Canadians storm the jail at Niagara-On-The-Lake where he is being held before being deported to the United States and free him.

1840 The British American Institute is opened in Dresden, Ontario, by Josiah Henson as a refuge for escaped slaves.

1846 The court decision is handed down on the *Dred Scott vs. Sandford* case. Scott was a slave who sued his owner for his freedom with the help of his White friends since his previous owner had let him live in the free territories of Illnois and Minnesota. The jury decids in his favour, but the state Supreme Court rules against him. The decision is appealed to the Supreme Court but the Court rules that Scott must remain a slave as he lacks standing in court because as a slave he is not a "citizen" and consequently has no rights of citizenship. The Court ruling also means that Congress has an obligation to protect the property of slaveholders.

1847 Blacks in Canada meet to discuss their common concerns at the Convention of the Colored Population at Drummondville.

Frederick Douglass begins publication of the *North Star* in Rochester, New York, as an anti-slavery newspaper.

1849 The community of Buxton, in the township of Raleigh, near Chatham, Ontario, is established by Reverend William King as a settlement for escaped slaves.

1850 The second Fugitive Slave Law is passed in the United States putting all people of African descent at risk of re-enslavement and a strong temptation to kidnap free Blacks is fueled. The Act denies alleged fugitives a trial by jury and provides payment for the capture of a slave, and citizens can be required to assist in capturing slaves, with penalties of imprisonment of up to six months and a fine of $1000 for not assisting.

The Common Schools Act is passed in Ontario, providing for the establishment of segregated schools.

1851 Delegates of the North American Convention of Free Colored Men meeting in Toronto on September 11–13 decide that Canada is the preferred location for Black emigration from the United States.

The Anti-Slavery Society of Canada is formed in Toronto to assist escaped slaves.

Henry Bibb, a former slave, and his wife Mary begin publication of the *Voice of the Fugitive* in Windsor, Ontario, promoting assistance to freedom seekers.

1852 A race riot occurs in St. Catharines, Ontario, resulting in the levelling of homes of many Black residents by Whites who are opposed to them.

1853 Mary Ann Shadd founds, edits and publishes the *Provincial Freeman* in Canada and becomes the first Black woman publisher in North America.

1861 The American Civil War begins. With the beginning of the war, the Underground Railroad virtually ends.

1863 On January 1, President Lincoln signs the second Emancipation Proclamation, declaring abolition in parts of the United States that are still in rebellion.

1864 During the Civil War, Black soldiers are massacred following their surrender in Tennessee.

1865 With the end of the war, slavery is abolished throughout the United States through the 13th Amendment of the Constitution. This amendment states, "Neither slavery nor involuntary servitude, except as a punishment for crime whereof the party shall have been duly convicted, shall exist within the United States, or any place subject to their jurisdiction."

The American Civil War ends with the signing of the terms of surrender of the Confederate states at Appomatox on April 9. With the end of the war, many people of African descent in Canada return to the United States to be reunited with family members.

The Reconstruction period begins in the United States following the end of the war.

Genealogy

The Harriet Tubman Family

The study of genealogy is the study of the descent and relationships of families. Some families are able to trace their families back for many generations to the grandparents of their grandparents or further, while others know more about the present, who their children and grandchildren are. Unfortunately, Black families, especially those outside Africa, are limited as to how far in the past they can trace their family backgrounds. Once enslaved, few records were kept of a person. The heritage of many Black families has been lost along with information identifying their African names or place of birth.

The enslavement of African people from 1400 to the abolition of slavery in the United States by 1865 resulted in some 20 million Africans being torn from their homeland and from their connections to each other. Not only were family names lost, but relationships with village neighbours were shattered and forgotten. The history of the African community of the enslaved persons was lost as they were forced to work and live with people brought from different parts of Africa to the New World.

Marriage records did not always exist for slaves, and if children were born, they might not be given the surname of their own father since as a slave, he had no rights recognized by law. Slaves were usually given the surname of the person who owned them like a brand to identify the slave as his family's property. Later slaves who were granted or gained their freedom might change their surname to confuse slave catchers or to reflect their new identity. This increases the difficulty in establishing the link between people.

The Author's Investigation of Harriet Tubman's Family

In order to trace the family legacy of Harriet Tubman in addition to her historical legacy, I began an investigation of Tubman's family tree. I was fortunate to be assisted in my research on both sides of the border and I found several family members. After meeting and interviewing a Canadian descendant, Betty Browne, I made contact with an American descendant, Mariline Wilkins. While both knew of each other, they had not met previously.

Upon learning that I planned to visit Mariline, Betty offered to join me. In Philadelphia, the two cousins faced each other for the first time. Our initial meeting took place in Mother Bethel A.M.E. Church. While the family resemblance was not immediately noticeable, they both possess a determination and interest in the legacy of their common ancestor Harriet Tubman. And, like Harriet, they are strong and independent women. Together, we met historian Charles Blockson at Temple University and reviewed some of the resources of the Blockson Afro-American Collection.

A year later, I was able to meet and interview many of Harriet Tubman's descendants at the Tubman Family Reunion. Each person had a special piece of the family puzzle which helped me to construct several genealogical charts.

These charts are based on information provided to the author by family members. They are not complete and do not represent the entire Tubman family. Certain documents and death certificates do not exist for African Americans until after the 1880s. Some freedom seekers gave themselves new names or married and sometimes the same family name is spelled in different ways. Consequently, information on familyís history can not readily be confirmed and oral histories, letters and family bibles provide the basis of these charts.

For more contemporary relatives of the Tubman family, some people were not named because of divorce or because names were not remembered. For these charts, information was provided by family members at the Tubman Family Reunion. Information on both Mariline Wilkins and Betty Browne was provided by their stories and other documents. These charts, therefore, primarily represent the descendants who gathered together for a reunion in Rochester and the cousins who were reunited in Philadelphia. Any errors or omissions related to this method of data collection are completely unintentional.

While these charts have more personal value to Tubman family members, I am including them to ensure that the family connections of one well known person of African descent are not lost. Future writers of Black Genealogy or Black History may find them useful tools. Many others may also find them of interest since the family of Harriet Tubman provides a rare example of a Black family that can trace it's origin back to Africa and include present day people from across North America.

Guidelines for Creating a Genealogy

Creating a family chart will require all of your investigative skills. A family tree charts the relationships within a family in a clear and concise way. It is important to record and date all the information that you have. A family tree branches out or becomes bigger and more complex as cousins are added. You should focus on just one branch of your family at a time. It does not provide a lot of descriptive information, but family stories or photographs could be kept in a family scrap book.

Often with families of African descent there will be more information available through the mother's side of the family. Start with your mother, then her parents, then her grandparents and so on. Later repeat the process with your father's family. You should be trying to find out the name (including nicknames) of the person, the date and place of their birth/death, and their relationship to you. If you find out more details you might discover that you share some trait, talents or interests with your ancestors.

Chart as much of your family history as you can, including grandparents and great grandparents. If you are unable to find a name for someone, you could place a question mark (?) a "Y" for a male and an "X" for a female in that space until you are able to find out the name in the future; an "m" indicates "married to." For example, the following is the chart for Harriet Tubman:

Harriet Tubman Ancestors

In this chart, Harriet is placed in relation to her parents, her grandparents and her siblings. Her ancestors were from Africa. Harriet had no children of her own, and therefore has no direct descendants. However, she did have brothers and sisters and some of them did have children. Hence, Harriet had nieces and nephews who would continue the family legacy.

The chart shows where we can begin to look. The best place to start is to interview relatives to gain whatever information they have about your family. While you can go to archives, churches, historical societies and special library collections for information, talk to older family members or even older family friends first since they can provide you with helpful clues. Records of birth, employment or military activity help to provide important details, but often such records were made some time after an event and the information can be incorrect and will need to be confirmed.

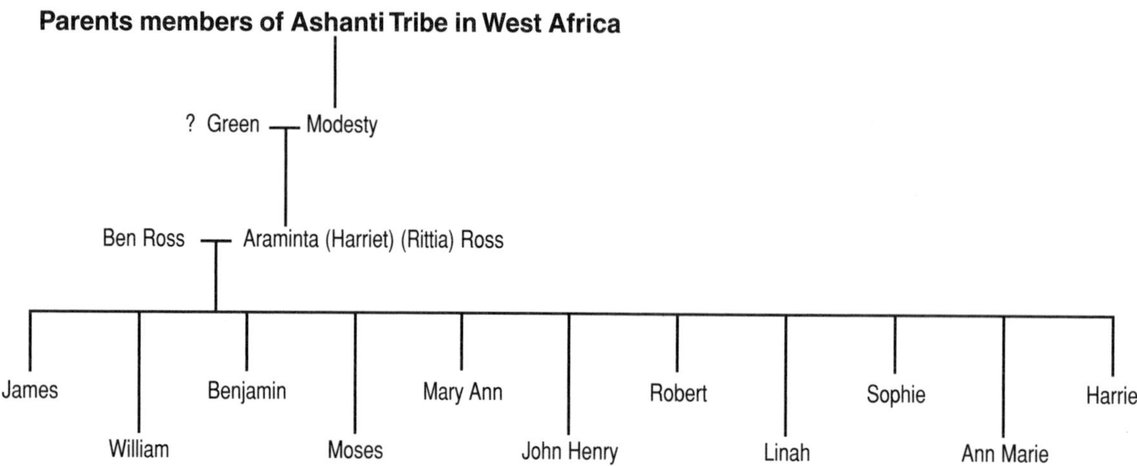

Betty Browne, Mariline Wilkins Charles Blockson and Rosemary Sadlier in Philadelphia.

When Harriet Tubman's newly freed family came to Canada, many of her brothers and sisters changed their surnames to Stewart, the surname of their father's (Benjamin Ross) last owner.

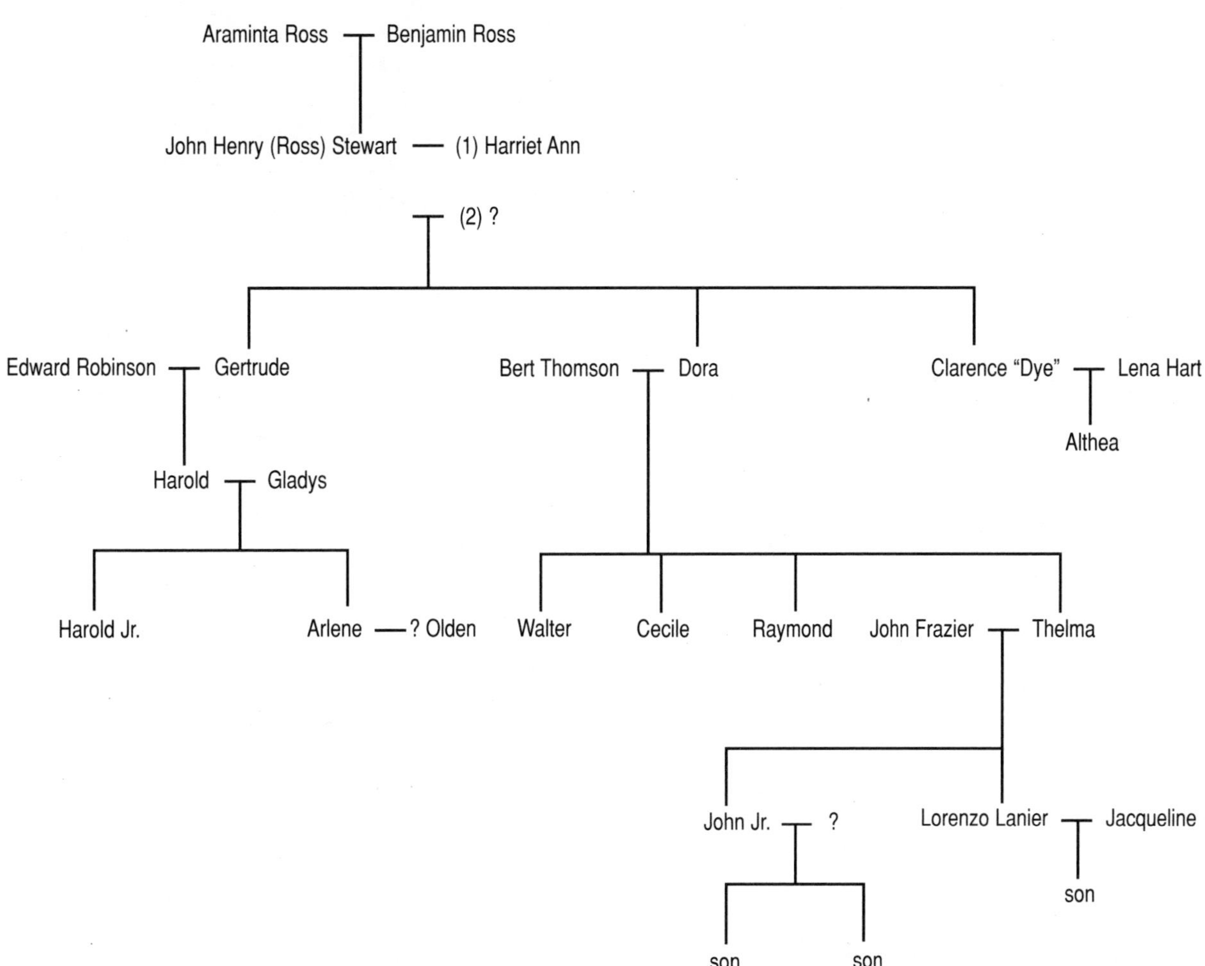

Reuniting Cousins

In Philadelphia, I was able to reunite one American branch of Harriet Tubman's family with a Canadian branch. Mariline Wilkins and Betty Browne are the descendants of "Aunt Harriet" through Harriet's brothers James and William.

Descendants of James & William (Ross) Stewart (Harriet's brothers)

It is interesting to note that Mariline's mother, Eva, was born in St. Catharines and later raised in Auburn, New York, by Harriet Tubman while Betty's family members of the Canadian branch were born and remained in Canada.

The Barnes Family, William Jr., Ollie, Cecil Lorne, Carrie.

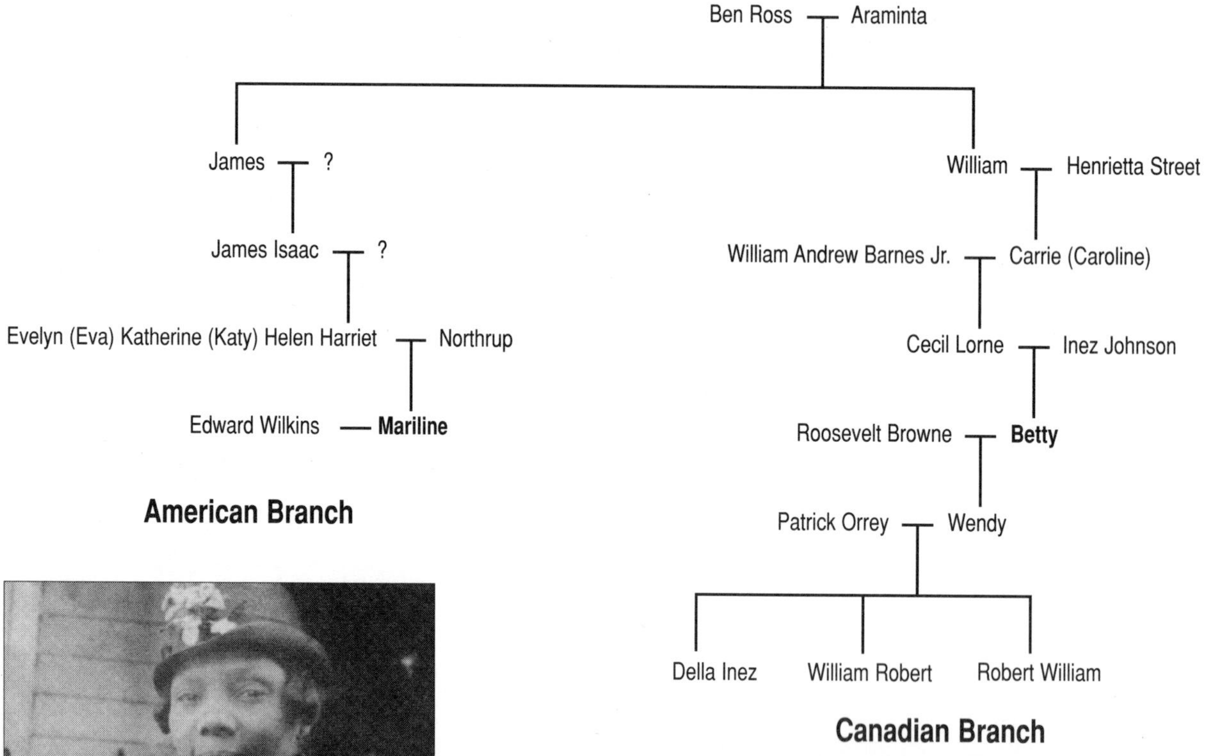

Ben Ross — Araminta

American Branch

- James — ?
  - James Isaac — ?
    - Evelyn (Eva) Katherine (Katy) Helen Harriet — Northrup
      - Edward Wilkins — **Mariline**

Canadian Branch

- William — Henrietta Street
  - William Andrew Barnes Jr. — Carrie (Caroline)
    - Cecil Lorne — Inez Johnson
      - Roosevelt Browne — **Betty**
        - Patrick Orrey — Wendy
          - Della Inez
          - William Robert
          - Robert William

Carrie Barnes's sister Martha of Niagara Falls

Carrie (Caroline) Barnes and Henrietta (Street) Stewart, daughter and mother in St. Catharines.

The Family Reunion

From my discussions with family members at the Tubman Family Reunion, the following chart shows the intricate network of relationships for some of Harriet Tubman's other known descendants who live across North America.

Henrietta (Street) Barnes, who relates the story of the escape to freedom of her parents in "The Escape Story" on page 45.

This chart traces the ancestors of Betty Barnes through her mother's side.

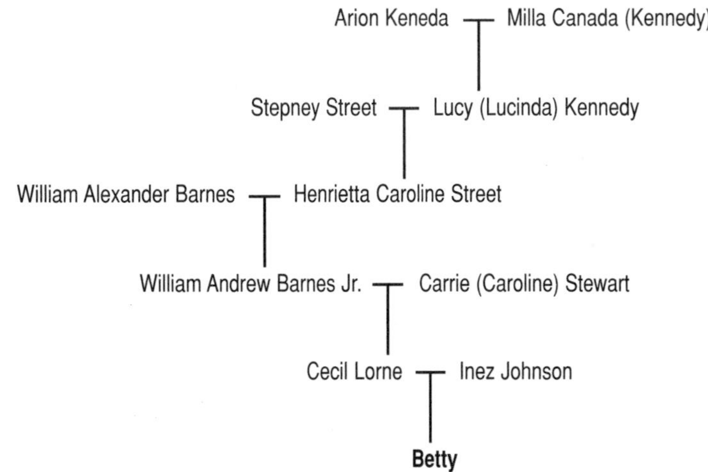

Carrie Stewart. Carries sisters were Amanda, Martha, Gertrude and Mary

Descendants of Ann Marie (Ross) Stewart

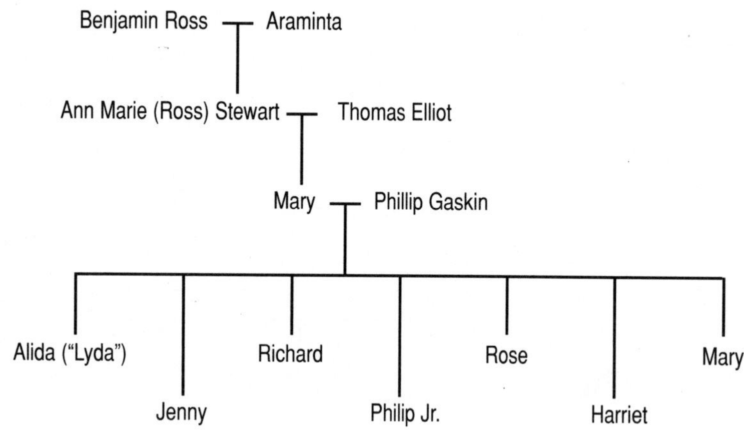

(see page 87 and 91)

Descendants of Alida (Lyda) Gaskin / (Harriets niece)

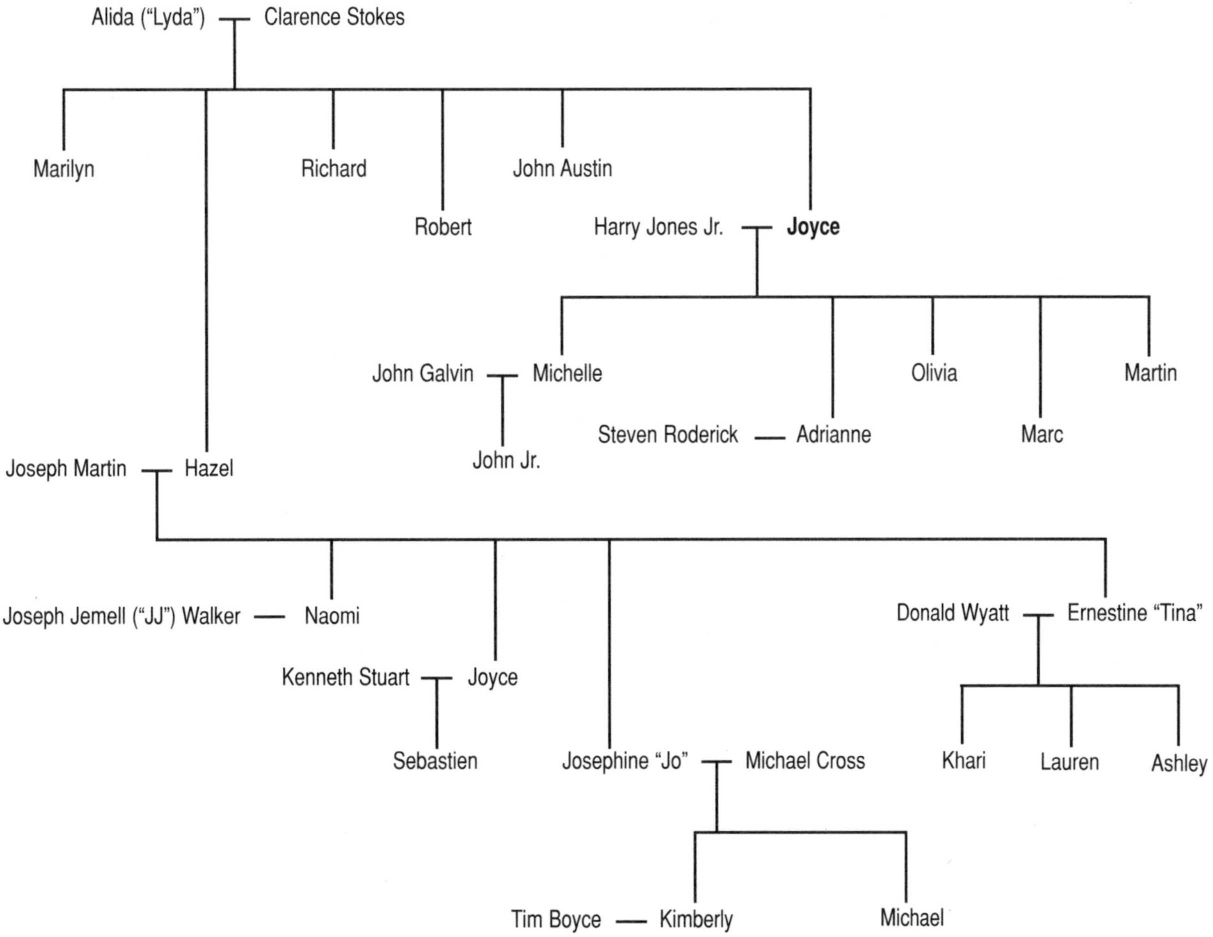

Alida ("Lyda") — Clarence Stokes

- Marilyn
- Hazel — Joseph Martin
  - Joseph Jemell ("JJ") Walker — Naomi
  - Kenneth Stuart — Joyce
    - Sebastien
  - Josephine "Jo" — Michael Cross
    - Tim Boyce — Kimberly
    - Michael
  - Donald Wyatt — Ernestine "Tina"
    - Khari
    - Lauren
    - Ashley
- Richard
- Robert
- John Austin
- Harry Jones Jr. — **Joyce**
  - John Galvin — Michelle
    - John Jr.
  - Steven Roderick — Adrianne
  - Olivia
  - Marc
  - Martin

Joyce Jones and Rosemary Sadlier

Descendants of Jenny Gaskin

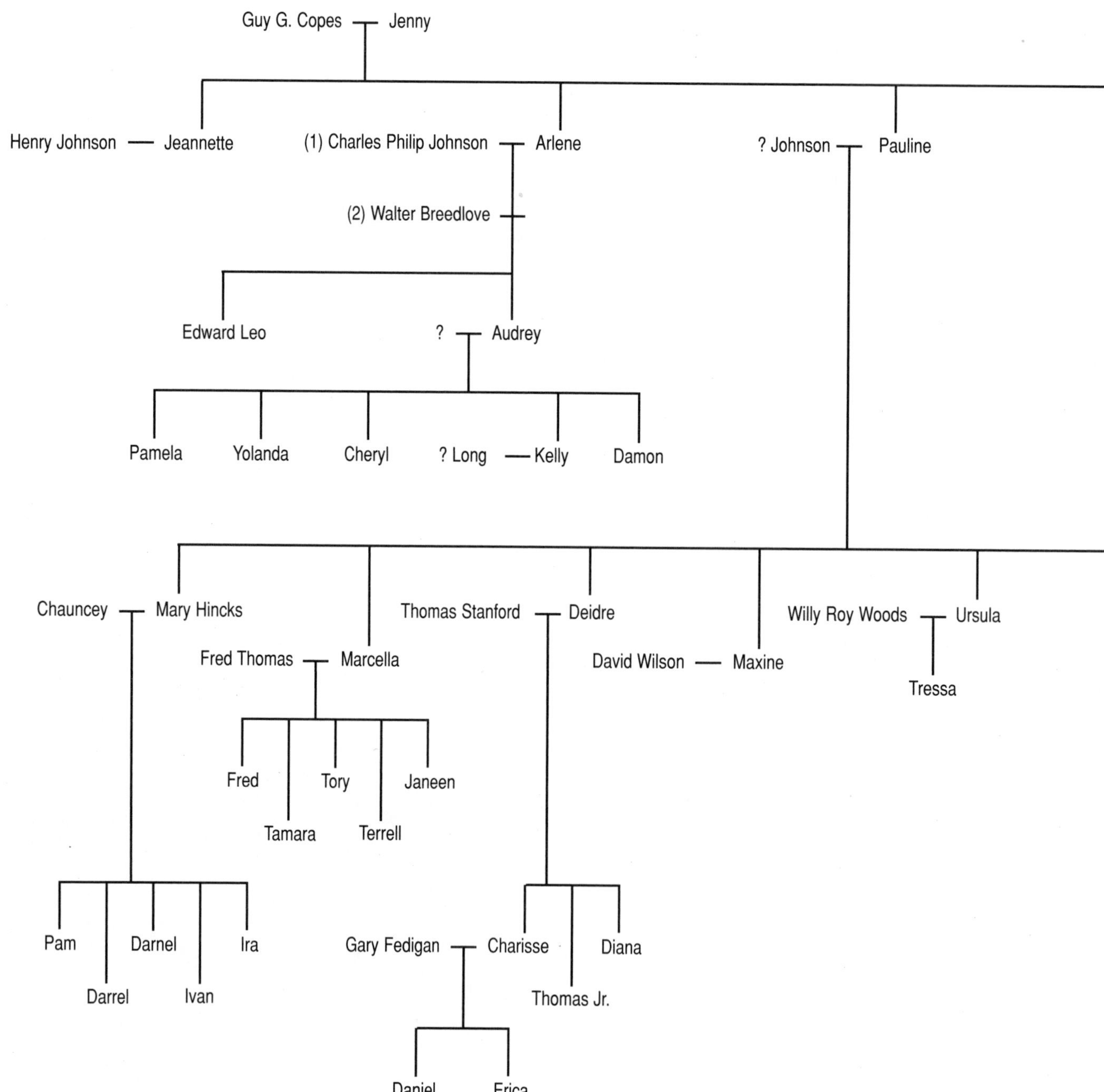

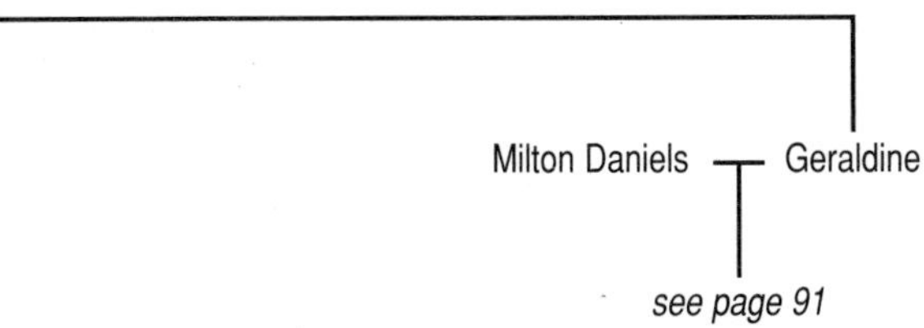
Milton Daniels
Geraldine
see page 91

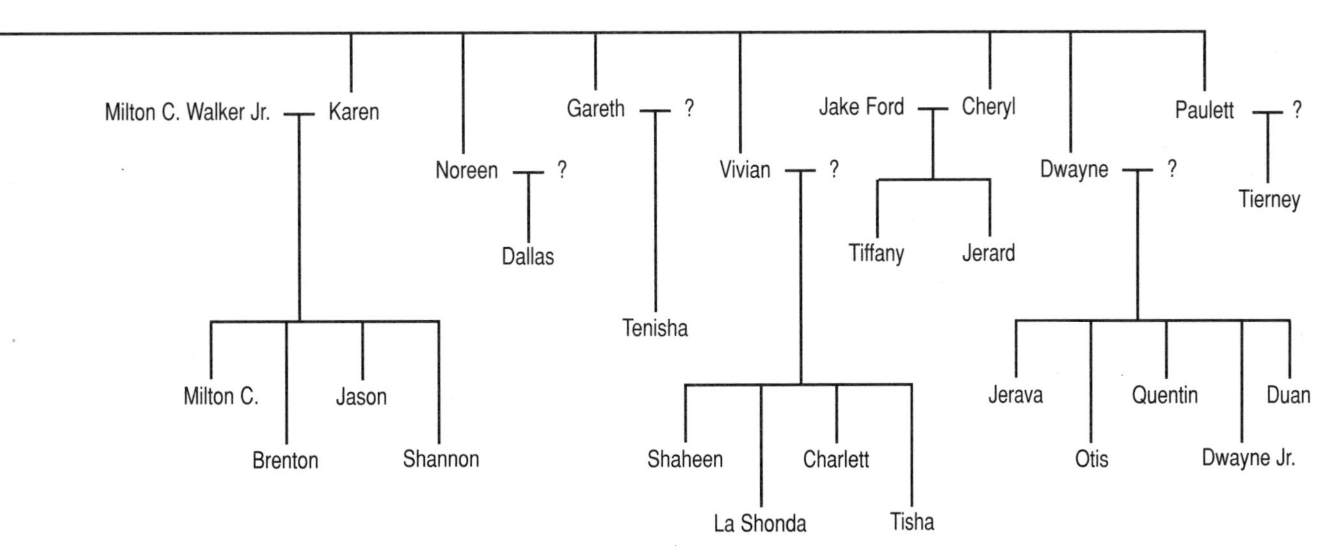
Milton C. Walker Jr.
Karen
Milton C.
Brenton
Jason
Shannon
Noreen
?
Dallas
Gareth
?
Tenisha
Vivian
?
Shaheen
La Shonda
Charlett
Tisha
Jake Ford
Cheryl
Tiffany
Jerard
Dwayne
?
Jerava
Otis
Quentin
Dwayne Jr.
Duan
Paulett
?
Tierney

Descendants of Jenny Gaskin

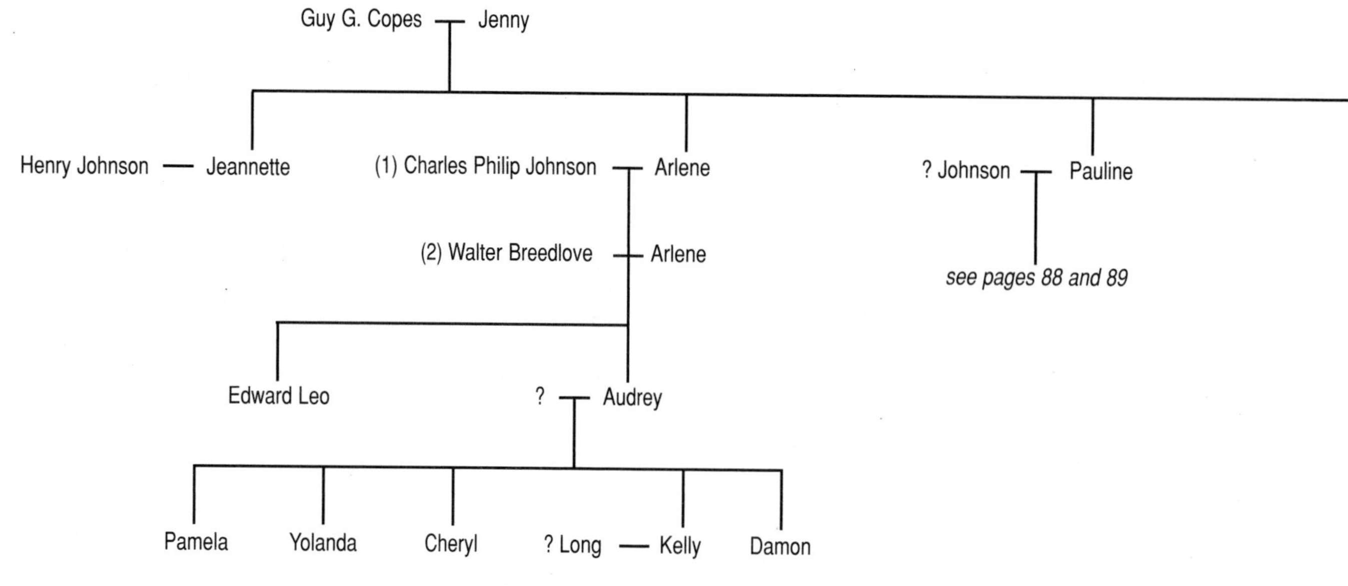

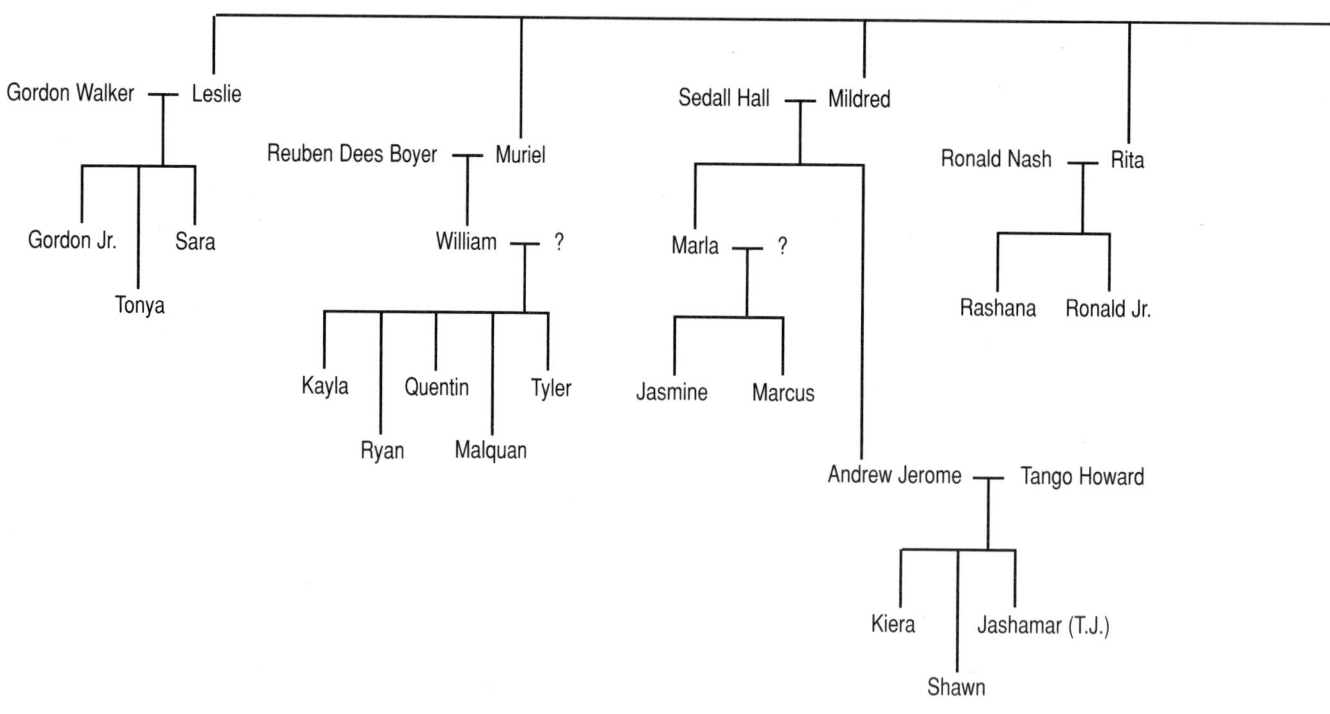

While your own family tree may not look like this, think of the work that you begin now like a small plant. Over time with your attention and care and the right conditions, it will grow. As you work on your family history, your knowledge of your ancestors will grow and your appreciation of their past, current and potential contributions to society will be affirmed.

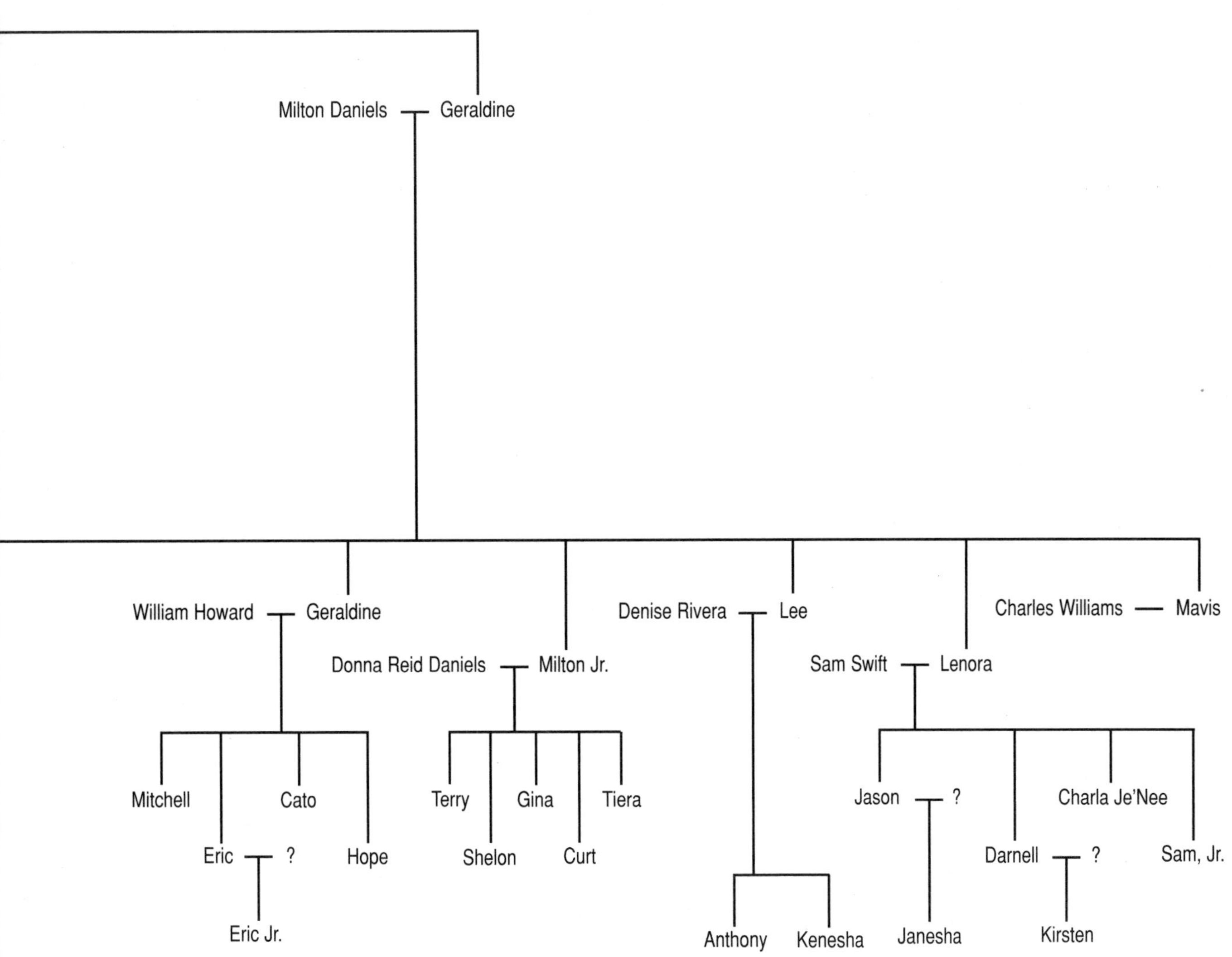

Further Reading

There are numerous references on Harriet Tubman in books, videos and films. The following books are generally suitable for young readers:

Adler, David A. *A Picture Book of Harriet Tubman.* New York: Holiday House, 1992

Bains, Rae. *Harriet Tubman: The Road to Freedom.* Mahwah, N.J.: Troll Associates, 1982.

Bentley, Judith. *Harriet Tubman.* New York: Franklin Watts, 1990.

Carlson, Judy. *Harriet Tubman: Call to Freedom.* New York: Fawcett Columbine, 1989.

Ferris, J. *Go Free or Die: A Story About Harriet Tubman.* Minneapolis: Carolrhoda, 1988.

Haskins, Jim. *Get on Board, the Story of the Underground Railroad.* New York: Scholastic Book Services, 1993.

Hill, Daniel G. *The Freedom Seekers: Blacks in Early Canada.* Toronto: General publishing, 1981.

Hill, Lawrence. *Trials and Triumphs: The Story of African Canadians.* Toronto: Umbrella Press, 1993.

Humphreyville, Frances T. *Harriet Tubman: Flame of Freedom.* Boston: Houghton Mifflin, 1967.

McClard, Megan. *Harriet Tubman: Slavery and the Underground Railroad.* Englewood Cliffs, N.J.: Silver Burdett, 1991.

McGovern, Ann. *"Wanted dead or Alive": The True Story of Harriet Tubman.* New York: Scholastic Book Services, 1965.

Meyer, Linda D. *Harriet Tubman: They Call Me Moses.* Seattle: Parenting Press, 1988.

Polocovar, Jane. *Harriet Tubman.* Chicago: Childrens Press, 1988.

Sadlier, Rosemary. *Leading the Way: Black Women in Canada.* Toronto: Umbrella Press, 1994

Taylor, M. W. *Harriet Tubman.* New York: Chelsea House, 1991.

The following references are useful for more advanced reading:

Blockson, Charles. *Hippocrene Guide to the Underground Railroad.* New York: Hippocrene Books, 1994.

Blockson, Charles. *The Underground Railroad, First Person Narratives.* New York: Prentice Hall, 1987.

Bradford, Sarah. *Scenes in the Life of Harriet Tubman.* Secaucus, N.J.:Citadel Press, 1961 (reprint)

Conrad, Earl. *Harriet Tubman.* New York: Eriksson Press, 1943.

Drew, Benjamin. *The Refugee or a North-Side View of Slavery.* Boston, 1856.

Quarles, Benjamin. "Harriet Tubman's Unlikely Leadership" in *Black Leaders of the Nineteenth Century,* edited by Litwack, L. and Meir, A.. Chicago: University of Illinois, 1988.

Hill, Daniel G. *The Freedom Seekers, Blacks in Early Canada.* Toronto: General Publishing, 1981.

Jackson, John N. and Wilson, Sheila. *St. Catharines, Canada's Canal City.* St. Catharines: The St. Catharines Standard, 1992.

Ripley, C. Peter, ed. *The Black Abolitionists Papers, Volume 11, Canada 1830–1865.* Chapel Hill, N.J.:University of North Carolina Press, 1986.

Sadlier, Rosemary. *Leading the Way: Black Women in Canada.* Toronto: Umbrella Press, 1994.

Silverman, J. *Unwelcome Guests: Canada West's Responses to American Slaves, 1800–1865.* Millwood, N.Y.: Associated Faculty Press,

Still, William. *The Underground Railroad.* Chicago: Johnson Publishing Company, 1970.

St. Catharines Journal, various issues, 1826–1865.

St. Catharines Centennial History. St. Catharines, Ont.: Advance Printing Ltd., 1967.

Thomas, Owen, *Niagara Freedom Trail.* Niagara Falls, Ont.:The Region Niagara Tourist Council, 1995.

What's Up Niagara Magazine. Niagara Falls, October 1993.

Winks, Robin. *Blacks in Canada: A History.* Montreal, P.Q.: McGill-Queens University Press, 1971.

Index

Credits

Betty Browne Collection, (all) 84; Harriet Tubman Home, 62; Metropolitan Toronto Library Board, 8; Norval Johnson Heritage Museum, Niagara Falls, ON., 23; Ontario Black History Society, 7.16, 17, 20, 25, 34, 59, 63; Rosemary Sadlier 31, 58, 65, (from Harriet Tubman Home) 66; (all) 67; (all) 68; 73, 82, 85, 87, (from Harriet Tubman Home) 66 (*top*); St. Catharines Historical Museum, 39, 41, 49, 61; St. Catharines Museum, 43, 66 (*bottom*); Niagara Falls Heritage Collection, Niagara Falls, Public Library, (all) 53; Cayuga County Historian, 69, 70, 71, 74; Umbrella Press, 47, (all) 56.

...It is appropriate that the city give official recognition of the passing of this wonderful woman. No one of our fellow citizens of late years has conferred greater distinction upon us than has she. I may say that I have known "Aunt Harriet" during my whole lifetime. The boys of my time always regarded her as a sort of supernatural being; our youthful imaginations were fired by the tales we had hear of her adventures and we stood in great awe of her. In later years, I came to know her more intimately through the relations of business. She was a women of unusual judgment and great common sense. Her integrity was never questioned . She was slow to make a promise, but once made, she was scrupulous to fulfill it to the letter. She was a woman of deep religious convictions and she has told me over and over again of her faith in the Master and of the certainty that she would find a place by His side in her eternal home. She seemed to intersperse her ordinary conversations of life with fitting quotations from the Scriptures and who can say that it was not this faith in divine providence which gave the vital force to the successful termination of her marvelous undertakings in behalf of her people.

Greatness in this life does not come to people through accident or by the caprice of fate or fortune; it is the reward of great zeal accompanied by great faith in the object sought and the persistent fighting against great obstacles and difficulties for its accomplishment....

Eulogy by John P. Jaeckel,
President of the Common Council of the city of Auburn, New York,
at the funeral of Harriet Tubman